Frank —
See you on
the road!
Jack

Joyrides Around San Diego

FROM THE SEA, TO THE MOUNTAINS, TO THE DESERT, YOUR GUIDE TO FINDING NEW JOURNEYS

By Jack Brandais

JOYRIDE GURU ®
SAN DIEGO, CALIFORNIA

Edited by Jennifer Silva Redmond.

Cover and logo design by Jennifer Proud.

Book design by Jack Brandais.

Maps created using an Automobile Club of Southern California base map. Used with the permission of the Automobile Club of Southern California.

The author has made every effort to provide accurate, up-to-date information and accepts no responsibility for loss, injury or inconvenience sustained by any person using this book.

Joyride Guru® on Facebook: facebook.com/weekenddriver

Joyride Guru® on Twitter: @joyride.guru

Joyride Guru® on Instagram: @joyrideguru

Contact the author through his website, http://www.joyride.guru

All of the Joyride Guru® drives are available on Amazon Kindle.

Joyride Guru® is a registered trademark of Jack Brandais.

Amazon, Kindle, and all related logos are trademarks of Amazon.com, Inc. or its affiliates.

ISBN-13: 978-0-692-79050-2 • ISBN-10: 0-692-79050-0

Library cataloging data available on request.

ON THE COVER: A motorcyclist enjoys a near-sunset drive on Sunrise Highway.

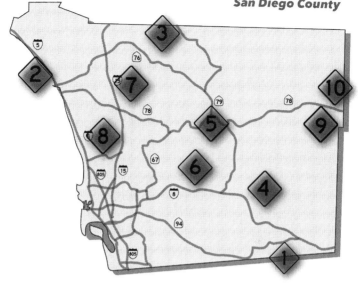

San Diego County

Joyrides Around San Diego

TABLE OF CONTENTS

v

Old Highway 80.

Introduction

THE OPEN ROAD APPEALS TO ALL OF US; HERE ARE 10 DRIVES WHERE YOU CAN FIND IT

FUNNY THING ABOUT the open road.

Everything from car commercials, to finding-yourself novels, to inspirational posters uses images of beautiful, empty highways.

The road trip is an adventure for the family, or a romantic drive before there's a family.

Yet even when great, empty patches of pavement are just a few minutes away, humans tend to stick to what they know and what everybody else knows.

They head for the crowds.

San Diego County is a big place, with more than three million people, covering an area almost as big as Connecticut. Most of us live on or within a few miles of the Pacific Coast; the eastern parts of the county are mountains and deserts. Development is difficult because of a variety of factors, including the sometimes rugged terrain and a lack of water.

For those of us who are looking for the roads less traveled and enjoy driving, it's an ideal place.

Did you read that right? What's there to enjoy about driving? Sitting on the freeway for hours, running to the store, spending more of life in our car than we spend in our living room?

No. I hate traffic. That's why I've spent time looking for twisting, curving, wide-open routes practically since I got my driver's license.

The mountains, valleys, and deserts do have a few residents connected by roads. These roads are what I've been writing about since the early 1980s, and continually since 2000, when I started writing the "Weekend Driver" column for Mark Maynard at the *San Diego Union-Tribune*. In 2003, *Weekend Driver San Diego*, a collection of columns, was published by Sunbelt Publications.

Each of the drives in the Joyride Guru series is fresh, with new information, and new insights into these journeys.

I guess I come from a line of folks who had the courage to make a left turn when everybody else went right. My Swedish maternal grandfather, who passed away long before I was even born, was, by all accounts, the first in the family to leave his tiny fishing village in Sweden, and journey to the United States.

He left Sweden sometime around World War I, wandering around the U.S. for a few years, until he found San Diego. His record picks up here in 1918. It was a time when fishing meant taking little boats out into the Pacific in search of big fish. Much of that time he spent alone.

My maternal grandmother, who was my only grandparent still

A bike day in the gold-rush era town of Julian.

Little Blair Valley in the Anza-Borrego Desert State Park.

alive when I was growing up, drove well into her 70s. She had driven thousands of miles on trips, sometimes alone. She always said driving—for pleasure—was one of her happiest experiences. My mom still tells tales of drives with her mom, brother, and sister, while her dad was out fishing. They visited Los Angeles and points beyond in a 1928 Oldsmobile touring car.

My dad emigrated here from France after World War II. It's a long story, but he finally made it to his destination, California, which he fell in love with while watching American movies in France. We'd take Sunday drives around the county, and summer driving trips all over California.

The planning—maps, research in tour books, writing for reservations at motels along the way—was one of my favorite activities.

There's a certain comfort level in going where everybody else goes. There's always someplace to eat, a restroom, and other people around to give a sense of safety and security.

One of the drives in this book, "Quintessential California," will give you that comfort level. It's a cruise down the original main road from San Diego to Los Angeles, the former U.S. 101 along the edge of the Pacific. South from Oceanside to Del Mar you'll drive, and it is plenty civilized. It's also a great break from Interstate 5, which can be a parking lot even on weekends.

At the other end of this big county is "Off the Grid Journey," which goes over county Highway S-2 in the desert. Although your route only goes a few miles south of Highway 78, drivers get a sense of what has been called the "loneliest road in San Diego County."

There's "Towering Old Highway" which seems deserted but only

Local residents at Carlsbad beach.

because it's been bypassed by Interstate 8, the freeway that's always only a few minutes away, should you get scared from all the quiet and open space.

And there are places to eat and restrooms on all these trips; I'll tell you where.

Whether your ride is a motorcycle, sports car, cheap compact, SUV, or minivan, take it easy, watch the curves, and be safe. Take some water and a few munchies with you; maybe throw a blanket in the trunk. Fill up with gas before you go.

Get out there and explore this county, whether you're a native, immigrant or visitor. You won't believe what's out there.

By the way, this book and the Joyride Guru series are a bit of an experiment. Each of these drives is available in individual format for digital download to—at this writing—the Amazon Kindle. The first ones were published in spring, 2015.

This print collection is for all of us who still prefer books on paper, and there are many advantages to that. It's difficult to flip through an electronic book, for example.

But there are advantages to the digital format. Since it's tied in with the Internet, the links are live. The Google maps you'll find with most of the drives are available with just a tap of the screen in the Kindle app.

I've made allowances so you, as a reader of this analog version, can still have all the digital material available. Just go to the URL *www. joyride.guru/booklinks* where you'll find a list of all the links mentioned in the paper edition.

And, a note on the maps. To fit in the format of this book, several deviate from the norm of having North at the top of the map; some of the long, east-west routes have West at the top.

Enjoy! And I'll see you on the road. Or maybe not.

Old highway east of Cuyamaca Junction.

Towering Old Highway

CLASSIC ROUTE AND ROADSIDE KITSCH ARE JUST OUT EAST

Forget driving to Route 66. The well-preserved former U.S. 80 in eastern San Diego County has all the charms of driving on an old country highway. Generally devoid of traffic, it has gentle curves with spectacular vistas in terrain ranging from high desert to mountain pines to California coastal hills. Desert View Tower is a must-see that isn't like anything on Route 66. And the freeway you take to get there isn't bad, either.

Old highway has beautiful vistas.

⟨⟩ Your Journey

DESPITE NOSTALGIA, THE good old days aren't always as romantic as all that.

My strongest memory of riding on U.S. 80 in the pre-freeway days is what seemed to be an endless trip back from visiting Aunt Eva and Uncle Morris in Tucson, probably the early 1970s because Interstate 8 was still under construction.

I was in the back seat of the family's 1968 Pontiac Tempest coupe. When moving, every expansion joint in Old Highway 80's ancient pavement was transmitted through the fine Morrokide-vinyl-covered seats. Flickering on the AM radio was the San Diego Chargers football game, probably with Stu Nahan calling the play-by-play and the Chargers going "left-to-right on your radio dial."

Just before Descanso—where the then-new freeway started—something stopped the one lane of traffic and it was getting hot in the back seat. End of memory.

Traffic zooming east abandoned this strip (and the U.S. 80 nomenclature) by 1975. The only trips we took there were Sunday drives to Cuyamaca or Pine Valley. It was only later, after I got my license and began running road rallies in the Tempest (time-and-distance Friday Nighters that started at the San Diego Zoo parking lot) that I began to truly appreciate the old road.

Since 2006, U.S. 80 has been recognized as a historic highway by the state of California, a designation that means it's an official living and changing drive-through museum.

We're only going over a small part of the highway which ran more than 2,500 miles from San Diego Bay to Georgia's coast; this drive's twisting route runs from just over the Imperial County line to Flinn Springs. Visitors will see a unique stone tower, the requisite out-in-the-country views, some old buildings, and old pavement.

Except for one stretch from Descanso to Willows Road, it's still one mostly-continuous concrete and asphalt ribbon, bypassed by my favorite freeway, I-8. In several spots, old U.S. 80 ducks over or under I-8, neatly breaking into five chunks that can create one great driving day or multiple adventures.

Some practical stuff: Gas stations are rare after Alpine. Fuel is available in Descanso, Pine Valley, and, adjacent to the freeway, at the Golden Acorn Casino and Jacumba. These spots might be a dozen or more miles apart so be sure to start out with a full fuel tank in your vehicle, and bring water and a few munchies for yourself.

The Desert View Tower at the top of Mountain Springs Grade.

A Brief History

EVERY YEAR, THOUSANDS of nostalgia-seekers and worshipers of great roads head out to festivals and other events along old Route 66, the historic highway that ran from Chicago to Los Angeles. San Diego residents on this pilgrimage might even take Interstate 8 east to southern Arizona before heading north to Kingman and other towns once served by U.S. 66.

As they fly past the San Diego County line at 75 miles per hour on I-8, they're missing a stretch of road that has all the attributes of old Route 66, except Bobby Troup's song, a TV show, and a lot of promoters. When U.S. 80 in San Diego and Imperial Counties was replaced by I-8, communities like Jacumba were frozen in time, just like many along old Route 66. Today, parts of once-busy U.S. 80 are among the loneliest roads in San Diego County.

Before the federal government started numbering highways in 1926, boosters in towns around the nation formed highway associations to select routes and create a system of "National Auto Trails" with romantic names. This road had several, including Old Spanish Trail, The Broadway of America, Dixie Overland Highway, and Bankhead Highway.

Old pavement west of Bankhead Springs.

Colonel Ed Fletcher of San Diego (Fletcher Hills) was very active in promoting driving routes, including helping fund a plank road through the Imperial County sand dunes. He was an active cheerleader with his fingerprints all over National Auto Trails routes in San Diego.

"Fletcher was an outspoken booster for highway development,

1917-vintage bridge once carried all east-west traffic.

particularly for roads to connect San Diego with the east," according to the 1936 *History of San Diego County*, excerpted on the San Diego History Center website. "He made a well-publicized auto trip to Washington D.C. in 1915 that took 26 days. In 1926, just eleven years later, he promoted one to Savannah, Georgia, which took just under three days."

Once the government got involved, the Dixie Overland Highway route was selected for U.S. 80, becoming America's southernmost continent-spanning highway. Take that, Route 66... you only go as far as Chicago.

For a list of some of the histories written about U.S. 80, check in the Sites and Eats section.

Getting There

INTERSTATE 8 IS YOUR starting point, whether your journey begins in San Diego to the west, or the desert to the east. Today, Old Highway 80 has five main segments (listed from east to west): Jacumba to Sunrise Highway; Sunrise Highway to Descanso Junction; Willows Road and Alpine; and Dunbar Lane to Flynn Springs County Park.

Each is unique and easily accessible. If you get tired of the drive at any point, just drive a few miles further and you'll find an on-ramp to Interstate 8. Keep the remainder for another day.

The Tower and a Lonely Road

ONE OF THE FEW surviving examples of building-as-billboard is the Desert View Tower, the start of the east-to-west journey. The tower sits at the top of the Mountain Springs Grade, itself a wonder

Vintage entry sign to Cleveland National Forest.

of early 20th century highway construction.

Exit I-8 at In-Ko-Pah Park Road and follow the historic markers to an original section of old U.S. 80. While this was at one time the main route (note the ruins of garages and other buildings), today it ends at the Desert View Tower, which was on a spur off the original highway.

One of the great roadside attractions in America, the tower dates to the mid-1920s and provides a spectacular platform for viewing I-8, the Mountain Springs grade, Borrego Badlands, Imperial Valley, and beyond to the Salton Sea, Colorado River, and Arizona.

Today owned by San Diegan Ben Schultz, it's well worth the small admission charge to see the great view from the tower, plus the adjacent rock garden created in the 1930s by artist W.T. Ratcliffe. Schultz is eager to point out the sights, which include several generations of the highway visible from the tower.

Back on old 80, head west to Jacumba over one of the loneliest roads in San Diego County. Although just a few miles long, it's a nice, straight road that rises and falls with the hilly terrain. The sparse high-desert vegetation is framed by the rugged mountains surrounding this wide valley, home to the town of Jacumba.

Now well past its prime, hot springs and the railroad put this one-time Native-American settlement on the map back in the 1920s, when Hollywood stars such as Marlene Dietrich and Clark Gable would "take the waters" at the old Hotel Jacumba. Built by Bert Vaughn (who also built the Desert View Tower), the hotel burned in 1983. Today, the town has only about 500 residents but you can still soak at the Jacumba Hot Springs Spa and Motel down the street from ruins of the old hotel.

CRUISE UP RAILROAD AVENUE for a real surprise—the old Jacumba train station (now a private residence) and train yards for the Pacific Imperial Railroad, the latest group to try to restart freight service on what was originally the San Diego and Arizona Railroad. This was "The Impossible Railroad" that opened in 1919, running from downtown San Diego, through Mexico, and on to a connection with the Southern Pacific (now Union Pacific) in the Imperial Valley. I'm still trying to picture Marlene Dietrich arriving or departing from this station in, say, 1938.

Parked there are several old engines (vintage Electro-Motive) and some old passenger cars with fading Amtrak logos. Several old, wooden train coaches that look to be the original rolling stock from the San Diego and Arizona's debut in 1919 are also near the tracks. This isn't a train museum and the area isn't open to the public.

Back on Old Highway 80, head west and cross the San Diego and Arizona Railroad tracks on the "modern" bridge (built in 1928). Remnants of a 1915 bridge's abutment are visible on the west end. Road archaeologist Casey Cooper called this "the only stretch of old U.S. highway I know of where so much has been maintained in such perfect condition."

A few miles down the road is Bankhead Springs, named for U.S. Senator John Bankhead of Alabama. Not only was Bankhead con-

The old train station in Jacumba, now a private residence.

Heavy traffic through Bankhead Springs.

sidered the father of U.S. 80 and the "Broadway of America," he was grandfather to a real Broadway star, actress Tallulah Bankhead. The Bankhead Highway auto trail was named for him; it ran from San Diego over the later U.S. 80 route to Texas, then veered northeast to Washington, D.C. An old hotel still stands here, but it is a private residence. Bankhead Springs is listed as a ghost town on the ghosttown. com website, although I think this is a bit of a stretch; there are people living there and it was never much of a town to begin with.

Next up as Old Highway 80 twists west is the town of Boulevard, where state Highway 94 splits south. Many of Boulevard's old buildings are still intact, including the Wisteria Candy Cottage, whose owners are the third generation to make homemade chocolates on site. There are a couple of convenience stores, so if you've become parched since Jacumba, stop in.

To stay on Old Highway 80 just west of town, keep right to county Highway S-1 at the wye with Highway 94. Old Highway 80 then meanders onto Live Oak Springs, one of the prettiest routes in the county.

Old highway meets new at the Golden Acorn Casino at Crestwood Drive. Operated by the Campo Band of the Kumeyaay Nation, the casino is a great spot to cool off on hot summer days. I'm not much of a gambler, but the restaurant here is OK—though I usually try to plan my food stop farther west in Pine Valley.

FOR DRIVERS WHO DON'T like curves, this is the best country road in the county. The last time this road was rebuilt, probably in the years immediately after World War II, engineers took out most of the hairpins and nicely banked the remaining curves. The result: a wonderful cruise, beautiful valleys, mountain passes, and generally very little traffic.

This is high-desert country, with the highway clinging to the hills above the valleys and ravines north of Campo. At 3,000-4,000 feet, this windswept area has a few ranches with horses and cattle. Look for the classic monument sign entering the Cleveland National Forest. The sign, and the one at the other end of the forest lands in Alpine, are great examples of "National Park Service Rustic" design, which in the early part of the last century strove to create buildings and other structures that blended in with their natural surroundings.

Wisteria Candy Cottage in Boulevard.

Beautiful downtown Pine Valley.

Pine Valley, Guatay, Descanso

AFTER PASSING A BORDER Patrol checkpoint near the real ghost town of Buckman Springs (there's really nothing left of what was once a mineral-water-bottling factory), you'll end up at Interstate 8 and Sunrise Highway, which goes to Mt. Laguna. Make the left turn just after crossing the freeway and drop into the little mountain town of Pine Valley, where there are several restaurants.

Pine Valley is a wonderful spot that, yes, has many pine trees. The highway is now on the west side of the mountains where the ecosystem is a bit wetter; on average they get about double the rain that falls in downtown San Diego or Jacumba, plus snow almost every winter. There are a couple of motels and bed-and-breakfast inns in the area in case you want to make a night of it.

A requirement for a country cruise is a stop at a local diner, and Major's Diner in Pine Valley fits the bill perfectly. It's been around since Maurice Major opened up in 1959 and is currently run by John Souza. I never miss a trip to the drive-up or drive-through Frosty Burger on the west end of town, except when I'm full from a lunch at Major's. There's also a fine little park, the Pine Valley County Park.

West of Pine Valley, look for two classic bridges that cross Pine Creek. You'll be driving on the 1929 version; a 1917 version is just to the south and is now on private property.

Continuing west, the road meanders up and down some hills, with gentle curves and views of the lightly forested area. Most of all, there's the slap-slap-slap of the expansion joints in the old concrete roadway, music to an old-road freak's ears but an annoyance to that kid riding in the Tempest all those years ago.

This side of the route twists much more but the engineers did a similar job in keeping things gentle and easy to handle. At the top of one of those hills is Guatay, a small hamlet.

Descanso Junction remains a big intersection in this small pond of roads, where the route to Cuyamaca and Julian splits north. The town of Descanso is northwest over Riverside Drive, as is one of my other Joyride Guru drives, Chapter 6 in this book, *Curves, Dirt and Cuyamaca*. From the Cuyamaca Highway intersection to Interstate 8, this part of Old 80 is the southern end of state Highway 79.

Between Descanso Junction and Interstate 8 are two old bridges representing very different eras. Turn west onto Wildwood Glen Lane and cross the Sweetwater River on the substantial-looking bridge from 1951. It was built for U.S. 80 at a time when the plan was to widen the highway to a four-lane expressway across the mountains, smashing through the little towns. This bridge was to be one side of that highway.

After crossing the bridge, keep driving and you'll find a nearly abandoned section of old U.S. 80, heading to where Interstate 8 chopped it off in the '70s. Then turn around and return to Los Terrinitos Road, which is an even earlier alignment of old U.S. 80. Before rejoining Highway 79, you'll cross the historic 1917-vintage Los Terrinitos Bridge. Imagine all the traffic from San Diego to the east coast crossing this bridge for 40 years or so, including the very busy years of World War II. This spot is the end of about 44 miles of mostly original highway. Continue west on I-8 to the Willows Road exit.

Viejas, Alpine, Flinn Springs

PICK UP THE OLD ROAD AFTER exiting I-8 by turning right onto Willows Road. This alignment goes through the Viejas Indian

"New" Pine Valley Creek bridge dates from 1929.

Vintage look to water tower at Flinn Springs.

Reservation, with its bustling hotel, casino, and outlet center. On either side of the casino complex, the road is still much as it was. By the way, the trip I took with my folks in the Tempest didn't follow this route; by then, the Willows loop had been straightened, mostly following the path of I-8.

Cross I-8 again and follow Alpine Boulevard and Arnold Way through the community of Alpine. Look for the bookend of the Cleveland National Forest sign you saw way back near Bankhead Springs; the western sign is just west of the Ranger Station.

Even though it's become somewhat suburban (with suburban traffic), there are still bits and pieces of back-country charm which Alpine's residents enjoy. The original "downtown" is around the Alpine Boulevard and Arnold Way intersection, with towering eucalyptus trees. Both Alpine Boulevard and Arnold Way were once U.S. 80 alignments; the older Arnold Way route has more twists.

At Dunbar Lane, duck under Interstate 8 and make a quick left to Olde Highway 80 (note the "e" in "Olde") for more original pavement. This stretch meanders along the freeway, going under just east of Flinn Springs County Park, a delightful county park that's a popular wedding spot. Just west of the park was once Marshall Scotty's Playland Park, which entertained kids from 1956-83.

About That Freeway

THERE'S NO DOUBT THAT Interstate 8 is my favorite freeway in San Diego County—it winds through the foothills and the Laguna and Cuyamaca mountain ranges from El Cajon east to the Imperial Valley and the county line. It's the freeway I send tourists on if they really want to learn about our region. And it can be darn fun to drive… if you manage to avoid rush hour on the urban portions.

As much as Joyrides celebrates our region's twisting, curving, narrow roads, there's a rather large group that would never consider driving on them. Visiting with the Corvette Owners Club of San Diego a few years ago, the owner of a late 1950s car said he always read my newspaper column, but had to pick and choose the routes he took.

"With a solid axle, it's just not enjoyable taking the 'Vette on some of those twisting roads," he said.

Same goes for my late cousin, Sy. In his 70s and 80s, Sy was still driving and although his former-rental-car Nissan Sentra might have enjoyed the curves, Sy didn't. He liked driving in a straight line, no matter where the road went.

Much of Interstate 8, once you pass Alpine, is outside of urban San Diego County. Those who built the Interstate system during its peak

This 1917 bridge is still open to traffic.

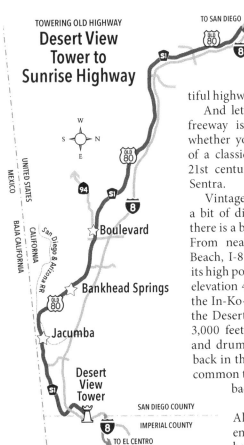

Desert View Tower to Sunrise Highway

TO SAN DIEGO

Pine Valley

Sunrise Highway

W
S N
E

TO SAN DIEGO

UNITED STATES
MEXICO

CALIFORNIA
BAJA CALIFORNIA

San Diego & Arizona RR

☆ Boulevard

☆ Bankhead Springs

☆ Jacumba

Desert View Tower

SAN DIEGO COUNTY

IMPERIAL COUNTY

TO EL CENTRO

construction years from the 1950s through the 1970s took a lot of pride in creating beautiful highways; I-8 is no exception.

And let's face it, a wide open freeway is a pleasure to drive, whether you're behind the wheel of a classic '50s car, a high-tech 21st century vehicle, or Sy's '93 Sentra.

Vintage vehicles might have a bit of difficulty on the trip, as there is a bit of climbing involved. From near sea level in Ocean Beach, I-8 rises and falls, hitting its high point at the Tecate Divide, elevation 4,140 feet. If you exit at the In-Ko-Pah Park Road exit for the Desert View Tower, you're at 3,000 feet. Overheated radiators and drum brakes were common back in the day; they'll be just as common today if you're driving a back-in-the-day car.

The Viejas Casino in Alpine is where suburbia ends and the open road begin. Just east is the Vista Point at an elevation of 2,900 feet. It honors early resident Charles Ellis, who arrived here in 1860. Ellis, and later his sons, developed a spring in the area. The view goes all the way to the ocean… if the sky is clear. Farther east is a large rest area at Buckman Springs Road.

The 400-foot high Pine Creek bridges were considered an engineering marvel when they were completed in 1974. Winds are such in the area that a windsock is at the west end of the twin spans; if you're in a high-profile vehicle, pay attention or you might go for an unexpected flight.

Something common to long-distance interstates is the wide median area, and I-8 is no exception. This is usually landscaped or left in its natural state, and provides a nice break between lanes.

Folks from flat states never imagine that we have mountains in San Diego. They'll marvel at the Tecate Divide, elevation 4,140. A few miles farther east is one of my personal favorites along I-8, the gentle curves through rugged Walker Canyon. This boulder-strewn area looks lunar, but the smooth freeway just plows right through, a testimonial to the engineers and construction workers that built it.

In case you decide to take a quick trip to the desert, keep going past the In-Ko-Pah Park Road exit to the Desert View Tower (but don't miss it on the way back). Continue east on I-8 to the Mountain Springs Grade, which snakes down the far side of the Jacumba Mountains into the Imperial Valley. The lanes have wide separation in this area, with bridges and steep cuts allowing the freeway to glide through the pink and brown rocks and cliffs. Look off to the side for older versions of the highway snaking around the sides of the canyon; the westbound lanes use some of the original right-of-way.

Once in the desert, I-8 is virtually a straight line for the rest of its trip to Tucson. Desert rats might disagree with me, but I find I-8 through San Diego County the most interesting part of the route and certainly the most fun to drive. Its gentle curves through the mountains and rocky high-desert areas are unique in the U.S.

And that's it. A full day of driving on a route I enjoy cruising in today's air-conditioned, Morrokide-free, backache-free, well-handling cars. The Tempest is long gone but I'm glad that old U.S. 80 is still there.

TO ALPINE, SAN DIEGO

Ellis Viewpoint
EASTBOUND ONLY

HISTORIC BRIDGES

Descanso

79

79

TOWERING OLD HIGHWAY

Sunrise Highway to Descanso

OLD 80

Guatay

W

S — N

E

HISTORIC BRIDGES

Pine Valley

S1

OLD 80

8

S1

TO BOULEVARD, EL CENTRO

TO MT. LAGUNA

Take the Trip

DISTANCE: About 54 miles (one way) from central San Diego on Interstate 8 from Flinn Springs County Park to the Desert View Tower. The return trip on the old U.S. 80 route is about 60 miles.

DIFFICULTY: Easy to moderate. Most of the serious hairpin turns were removed before the freeway replaced the two-lane highway in the 1970s.

DIRECTIONS

- Interstate 8 to In-Ko-Pah Park Road exit. Follow historic-site marker signs to northeastern portion of Old Highway 80.
- Return over In-Ko-Pah Park Road to freeway; use underpass to Old Highway 80.
- Keep right to stay on Old Highway 80 at wye junction with state Highway 94 in Boulevard.
- Cross Interstate 8 at Sunrise Highway.
- Left at Old Highway 80.
- Join Interstate 8 West at Japatul Road exit.
- Exit at Willows Road. Continue right.
- Cross Interstate 8 at Alpine Boulevard exit.
- Right after crossing freeway bridge to Alpine Boulevard.
- Left at wye intersection to Arnold Way.
- Left at Alpine Boulevard.
- Right at Dunbar Lane; go under freeway.
- Left at Olde Highway 80.
- Continue to Lake Jennings Park Road and Interstate 8.

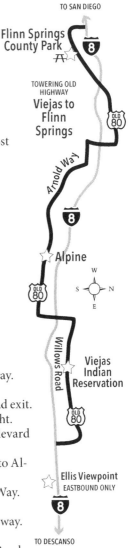

TO SAN DIEGO

Flinn Springs County Park

TOWERING OLD HIGHWAY

Viejas to Flinn Springs

Arnold Way

Alpine

Viejas Indian Reservation

Willows Road

Ellis Viewpoint
EASTBOUND ONLY

TO DESCANSO

For Nature Lovers

- Spectacular vista from Desert View Tower.
- Miles of high desert and mountain scenery.
- Hiking, camping, hot springs, and off-road trails abound.
- A vintage highway unique in Southern California.
- Some of the route is out of cellphone data range.
- Route is popular with bicyclists.

 Stuff for Adults

- Lots of nostalgia, whether or not you're from San Diego County.
- Hot springs in Jacumba.
- Wineries here and there along the route.
- Excellent for cruising in the vintage car, truck or motorcycle.
- Check your favorite online service for out-of-the-way lodging.
- Away from it all but an hour or less from home.

 Stuff for Kids

- Climb in Desert View Tower and the rock animal sculptures are fun (without electronics).
- Old trains to look at but not touch.
- Small, traditional parks in Pine Valley and Flinn Springs.
- Tiny chocolate shop in Boulevard.
- Constantly changing scenery.
- Hiking opportunities.
- They can experience another side of San Diego.

Sites and Eats

- *Find links to these web sources online at* www.joyride.guru/booklinks
- Jacumba Hot Springs Spa, motel, restaurant, spa; 44500 Old Highway 80, Jacumba, CA, 91934, (619) 766-4333.
- Wisteria Candy Cottage is a chocolate heaven, selling created-on-site goodies as well as many other types of candy; 39961 Old Highway 80, Boulevard, CA, 91905, (619)766-4453.
- Golden Acorn Casino is a modern anomaly in the sleepy Mountain Empire region; 1800 Golden Acorn Way, Campo, CA 91905, (619) 938-6049.

- Major's Diner is a bustling country cafe celebrating, and popular with, the car and motorcycle culture; 28870 Old Highway 80, Pine Valley CA, 91962, (619) 473-9969.
- Frosty Burger is a drive-up/drive-through with old-fashioned burgers, shakes and ice cream; 28823 Old Highway 80, Pine Valley, CA, 91962, (619) 473-9952.
- Pine Valley County Park, with picnic areas and kid play zones, open 9:30 a.m. to one half-hour before sunset; 28810 Old Highway 80, Pine Valley, CA, 91962, (619) 473-8558.
- Flinn Springs County Park is one of those neat spots tucked away off the freeway in what is now an area with industrial buildings; 14787 Olde Highway 80, El Cajon, CA, 92021, 9:30 a.m. to sunset daily; closed Christmas Day, (619) 561-0180.
- Keep an eye out for a few wineries along the way.

Flinn Springs County Park.

Old highway on the beach.

Quintessential California

COAST HIGHWAY HAS BEEN DELIGHTING TRAVELERS FOR MORE THAN A CENTURY

Get off of Interstate 5 and enjoy a drive through the coastal communities of Oceanside, Carlsbad, Leucadia, Encinitas, Cardiff-by-the-Sea, Solana Beach, Del Mar, and Torrey Pines. Depending on traffic, drive can be double the time of freeway travel but includes cliff-top and surf-side driving with spectacular vistas of the Pacific Ocean. Coastal communities' sites include "time warp" buildings, natural and historic sites, and side trips.

Looking south from Del Mar to Torrey Pines Beach as the Coaster heads north.

🪧 Your Journey

SURF AND SAND: IS there anything more Southern California than a beach drive? How about this description of San Diego County's Coast Highway from 1912:

"... One of the most delightful highways that an automobilist can find anywhere," wrote the anonymous author in the June, 1912, *Touring Topics*—then the magazine of the Automobile Club of Southern California. "The roadway closely follows the ocean shore, permitting to the traveler a splendid view of the Pacific on one hand and a constantly unfolding panorama of picturesque scenery on the other."

In the 21st century, that driver would certainly notice a lot of development but would still see the same "splendid view of the Pacific" in taking the nearly 25 miles on the old highway from Oceanside to Torrey Pines.

Known to locals as "Old Highway 101," county Highway S-21, and several different names in the small cities along the way, this was the main route between San Diego and Los Angeles for the first half of the 20th century. It parallels most of today's busy rail line (that dates to 1882) between the two cities. The highway has retained much of its charm and most of the frustrations that led to the building of the freeway: beautiful views and lots of stoplights. Is it worth the detour? Yes, especially since, at times, I-5 these days can have stop-and-go traffic along this stretch.

Like many of the old highways, Coast Highway is made to take at about 35 miles per hour. In the towns—Oceanside, Carlsbad, Leucadia, Encinitas, Cardiff-By-The-Sea, Solana Beach, and Del Mar—many vintage buildings remain from the 19th century up to the 1960s. John Daley, former co-owner of one of those buildings, the 101 Cafe diner in Oceanside, says the area is like a time warp.

"It's one of the three great drives in the United States," Dailey, an Oceanside native, said. "It's just an incredible drive. Not only do you have the physical beauty of the ocean, but you also have all these classic buildings that were built here in response to the road: the old drive-ins, the old service stations, the old hotels, the old auto courts.

"There's no question about it, we have almost all of our old buildings here that were built in the '20s, '30s, '40s, because when they moved the freeway away from us, everything just got caught in time."

I prefer to drive it from north to south, so I'm on the ocean side of the highway, but it's good in either direction. It's a straight shot from the Oceanside Harbor Drive exit off of I-5 to the end of this route, at I-5 and Genesee Avenue near UCSD. I'll give you a few detours and highlights along the way.

History

WHEN THE AUTOMOBILE came to California around the turn of the last century, drivers adventurous enough to take the trip from San Diego to Los Angeles followed a route generally along the then-Santa Fe Railroad tracks. Over the years, the trail grew into a paved road; when the federal government started numbering highways in 1926, it was designated U.S. 101, the main route between Los Angeles and San Diego until the 1964 completion of Interstate 5.

And, by the way, it's not the Pacific Coast Highway or "PCH." That

Beach and pier at Oceanside.

Cafe 101's been serving it hot since the 1920s.

route runs north from San Clemente and is mostly designated state Highway 1. Today, cities designate this coastal road as Coast Highway, Carlsbad Boulevard, Coast Highway 101, Camino Del Mar (in Del Mar), and Torrey Pines Road (in San Diego).

Beachfront Driving

THE BEST PARTS OF THE road are where the highway is actually on the sand or clifftop. When you first drive through Oceanside (on what was originally called Hill Street), you might wonder, "where's the beach?" Once you pass over the San Luis Rey River at the north edge of Oceanside, the Pacific doesn't make another appearance until just south of downtown Carlsbad. From there, it's on-and-off the coast for the next 20-plus miles.

Beach access is via stairs to Carlsbad State Beach. Street parking is available (if you can find it), with fee parking at the access area at the end of Tamarack Avenue. The vista is pretty great for drivers heading south, with views of the Agua Hedionda Lagoon. The road then dips into the lagoon basin, passes through a small developed area with homes on the beach side and past the massive Encina Power Station.

Just south of the Palomar Airport Road offramp (a remnant of a 1953 U.S. 101 bypass of Oceanside and Carlsbad) is a beautiful, three-mile stretch of beachfront driving along the South Carlsbad State Beach. There are a few places to park. The view is interrupted only by bluffs that hold a campground.

The highway ducks a bit inland through Leucadia and Encinitas, with a brief sea-view at Moonlight State Beach. It reemerges south of downtown Encinitas after passing the gold-domed Self Realization Fellowship Temple, at San Elijo and Cardiff state beaches. The north end is on the bluff and has a campground similar to Carlsbad's, then drops down to the mouth of the San Elijo Lagoon. Restaurant Row in Cardiff is a remnant of old roadside businesses, with a half-dozen restaurants on both sides of the street.

It's town views again through Encinitas and Solana Beach, before the mouth of the San Dieguito River puts us back on the beach at Del Mar. On the east side of the old highway is the historic Del Mar Race Track and fairgrounds, on the west is the Pacific. This is the beach made famous by the track's slogan, "Where the Turf Meets the Surf"; up to the 1980s or so, the thoroughbreds from the track would be walked under the highway and into the surf.

South of Del Mar is my favorite part of the route, Torrey Pines State Beach and Reserve. The bluffs on either side of the beach are higher, giving a more spectacular view of the surf. Look for the spray of the surf rising high in the sky.

Historic Towns

WHATEVER IT WAS CALLED, the official U.S. Highway designation meant a lot of traffic was going through your town. Relics from that era include Daley's former diner in Oceanside, opened in 1928, the next-door auto court, and across the street 1940s vintage auto dealers. In Carlsbad, you'll see the 1882 Carlsbad Water building and an 1886 vintage Victorian house that housed various restaurants, but is most remembered for its time as the Twin Inns.

Leucadia looks the most like it did in the old U.S. highway days,

Southbound Carlsbad Boulevard through South Carlsbad State Beach dates back to before 1930.

with its Log Cabin Motor Court and nearby Leucadia Roadside Park. The postage-stamp sized park is a remnant of many such public spaces that were built on the old highways. Motorists would use them as a spot to let the car's radiator cool down and perhaps have a picnic lunch. The public spaces were created because property owners were tired of drivers pulling into their fields for a rest.

Encinitas has restored and rebuilt its downtown with the historic La Paloma Theater and several blocks of vintage buildings. Legend has it that back in the old Hollywood studio days, the La Paloma was one of those theaters where producers would test an unreleased movie with audiences.

Cardiff-By-The-Sea's Restaurant Row is a remnant of the kind of roadside cafés and service stations that sprang up about where your Studebaker would need radiator water and gas. Solana Beach didn't have beach access because of the tall bluffs, so developer Ed Fletcher had the bluff washed away by a guy with a fire hose; the access is now called Fletcher Cove and it's at the foot of Lomas Santa Fe Drive. Del Mar started developing around 1910; the 1927 Stratford Square is a remnant of the town's original Old-English theme.

Parks, Camping, Nature, and Hiking

MOST OF THE BEACHES are managed by the State of California. Parking is sometimes free but there is only paid-parking inside the state beaches and on the street in Del Mar. Campgrounds are at the South Carlsbad, Cardiff, and San Elijo state beaches.

Torrey Pines State Reserve has a great old lodge at the top of a twisting grade that was originally the Coast Highway. Enter from the

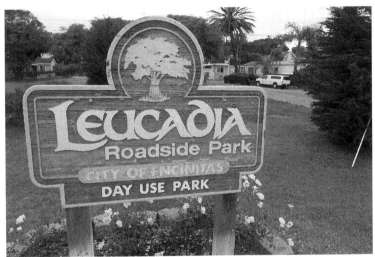

Leucadia Roadside Park is a relic from the past.

La Paloma Theater is a classic movie house.

beach at the bottom of the cliffs on the south side of the beach. Early cars had gravity-fed fuel, rather than a fuel pump — with their gas tanks generally behind the engine, cars such as Ford's Model T had to back up the grade. What fun.

The lagoons have visitor centers and foundations: Buena Vista, 2202 South Coast Highway, Oceanside; Agua Hedionda, 1580 Cannon Road, Carlsbad; Batiquitos Lagoon, 7380 Gabbiano Lane, Carlsbad; San Elijo, 2710 Manchester Ave., Cardiff-By-The-Sea. Much of the Los Peñasquitos Lagoon is inside Torrey Pines State Reserve.

Side Trips

THERE ARE A few spots along the way where it's fun to detour and explore the beach neighborhoods. For your journey, don't be afraid to just make a turn toward the ocean anytime there's development blocking your view. Hidden parks and coastal access points are all along the route. Here are my picks.

OCEANSIDE HARBOR AND BEACH: This charming little boat basin opened in 1963 and includes a number of restaurants, shops, and some boat and fishing charters in the Harbor Village development on the southwest side of the bay, while the northern shore has a couple of more restaurants. As you head down the hill from I-5, Harbor Drive splits; take the right turn to explore the north side, left to continue to the pier.

Go 'round about, through the coastal developments, to the Oceanside Pier, the sixth pier in the city, dating back to 1888. Watch for the dueling one-way traffic directions on The Strand that make driving especially confusing. Folks running around in swimsuits can also lead to driver confusion.

Continue south on North Pacific Street to explore the beach-

Historic route signs mark old highway.

front neighborhood, returning to Coast Highway at Wisconsin Street. On the corner you'll find the 1926-vintage 101 Cafe diner.

DOWNTOWN CARLSBAD: This quaint city's downtown is along Grand Avenue, the block north of Carlsbad Village Drive. Antique shops and restaurants are features of this very walkable area.

LEUCADIA: If you like, get lost on the confusing coastal streets in Leucadia. There's a bluff-top park above Beacon's Beach, 948 Neptune Avenue. Turn right at the tiny Leucadia Roadside Park at Leucadia Boulevard and twist around Neptune Avenue to the top. These are narrow streets, and Neptune is one-way going north, so have fun.

ENCINITAS BOAT HOUSES: Two homes in the 700 block of Third Street in Encinitas were built to look like they're dry-docked boats, even though they've never been on the water. Third Street is two blocks west of South Coast Highway 101, between West G and West F streets.

CARDIFF-BY-THE-SEA: In order to visit the small town, you'll have to go east across the railroad tracks. When I'm in the area, I always stop in at VG Donut and Bakery.

Take the Trip

DISTANCE: About 25 miles down the Coast Highway from Interstate 5/Oceanside Harbor Drive exit to the Genesee Avenue/Interstate 5 junction.

DIFFICULTY: Easy. Lots of stoplights. Wonderful route for the top down (if you have a convertible) and people-watching.

DIRECTIONS
- *See Google Map:* http://goo.gl/IHGfGx

- Interstate 5 to Oceanside Harbor Drive exit. Go west.
- Left at North Coast Highway. Road is the old U.S. 101, with several different street names through coastal cities. Watch for "Historic U.S. 101" posted throughout route.
- Left at Genesee Avenue near UC San Diego to Interstate 5.

Oceanside Harbor and Beach side-trip

- From Oceanside Harbor Drive and Interstate 5, continue through signal at Coast Highway. Follow Oceanside Harbor Drive as it turns left.
- At wye intersection, turn right for north side of harbor; left for south side and to continue on route.
- Continue south and west to shops and restaurants, and beach.
- When finished exploring harbor, take bridge over San Luis Rey River (North Pacific Street).
- Right at Surfrider Way to The Strand (note crazy one-way directions on The Strand, the road that parallels the sand.).
- Return to North Pacific Street when finished exploring beach. Right onto North Pacific Street. Continue south.
- Left at Wisconsin Avenue.
- Right at Coast Highway to continue route.

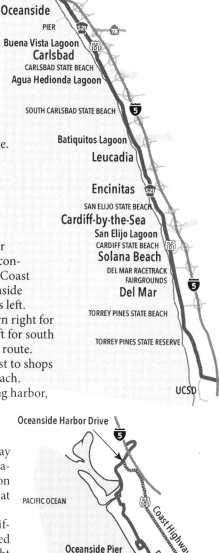

Oceanside Harbor and Beach Side-Trip
SEE DIRECTIONS FOR STREETS AND TURNS.

27

🐢 For Nature Lovers

- Six unique lagoons are along the way; stop along the way at visitor centers.
- Highway in many spots is right on the sand. Unparalleled views.
- It's the beach.

💡 Sites and Eats

- *Find links to these web sources online at www.joyride.guru/booklinks*

Keep some room for donuts at VG Donut and Bakery in Cardiff.

- Lagoon preservation groups: Buena Vista, 2202 South Coast Highway, Oceanside; Agua Hedionda, 1580 Cannon Road, Carlsbad; Batiquitos Lagoon, 7380 Gabbiano Lane, Carlsbad; San Elijo, 2710 Manchester Ave., Cardiff-By-The-Sea. Much of the Los Peñasquitos Lagoon is inside the Torrey Pines State Reserve.

- Historical Societies: Oceanside Historical Society; Carlsbad Historical Society; San Dieguito Heritage Museum; Leucadia 101 Main Street Association.
- 101 Cafe, 631 South Coast Highway, Oceanside.
- VG Donut and Bakery, 106 Aberdeen Dr., Cardiff.
- Cardiff-by-the-Sea Restaurant Row, 2500 block South Coast Highway 101, Cardiff-by-the-Sea. Check your favorite online review site.

Palomar Observatory.

Journey to the Stars

HISTORY, FRESH MOUNTAIN AIR ON THE ROAD TO PALOMAR MOUNTAIN

Wander up Palomar Mountain in northern San Diego County via two twisting paved roads or a historic dirt byway. Route passes an historic mission, an open-space park, agricultural areas, and casinos. The top of Palomar is a forested area, unique in the region. Good for kids and adults, but maybe not on the same trip.

Vista of Pauma Valley from near the top of South Grade Road.

⬡ Your Journey

MOUNTAIN AIR, TALL TREES, twisting roads, sometimes snow in the winter. Nothing like this in San Diego County, right? Not so. This alpine journey is right in our backyard: Palomar Mountain, on the county's northern border.

It's a great place for taking the kids on a country drive, the destination being the amazing Palomar Observatory. For the sport tourer—on two wheels or four—all the elements are there: twisting mountain roads, but not so twisty as to scare off commuters. And should you want some unpaved fun, a historic dirt road is one of the three ways to the top of the mountain.

Your journey can include stops at a very historic and genuinely Californian site, the Pala Mission, and a beautiful, isolated canyon in Wilderness Gardens County Park. Adults may enjoy the casinos operated by local Native American tribes for trips without kids.

Along the way

HEAD EAST FROM Interstate 15 over Pala Road, state Route 76, which generally follows the San Luis Rey River. You're driving to one of its headwaters, Mount Palomar, about 33 miles from I-15. This twisting, sometimes narrow road can have a great deal of traffic as gamblers head to the two casinos directly on our route, plus two or three others nearby. You're welcome to stop in, but make sure you don't gamble away the gas money or the pink slip to the car. Traffic is heavier in the afternoon and evening heading to and from the casinos, so a tip is to cover this part of the road early in the day.

Quickly, the highway gives drivers a taste of this area— San Diego County's agricultural center. Once there were a couple of dairies; today the old grazing lands are fallow or are growing vegetables, alfalfa, or other crops. A few old buildings still remain from the dairy days.

At Pala, the casino and high-rise hotel are hard to miss on the south side of SR-76. Easier to miss is the small town, which is north of SR-76; look for the signs. Mission San Antonio de Pala boasts that it is the only one of the original Spanish missions that continues to serve its original Native American community, the Pala Indians. The town and mission are located on their reservation. The town has a little store and a taco stand that has some great food. Dining in the casino across the street can be elegant and less adventurous, but the Mexican food is more authentic.

Pala Mission opened in 1816 as an *assistencia* (a branch church) to Mission San Luis Rey in Oceanside. The original buildings, courtyard, and cemetery are well worth the visit, offering a quiet look back at the style of California's early European settlements.

FROM PALA, CONTINUE east to the Wilderness Gardens Preserve, a county park with more than four miles of trails, picnic areas, and a historic site. It's located where Sickler's Grist Mill once stood, and the foundations, dating to 1881, are still visible.

In 1952, Manchester Boddy, *Los Angeles Daily News* owner/publisher and founder of Descanso Gardens in La Cañada Flintridge, bought the property as his retirement home. He died in 1967; the county took over the area in 1973 and has let it return to its natural

Mission San Antonio de Pala

state. Be aware that the park is closed in the month of August.

Our destination is the Caltech-operated Palomar Observatory, home to the 200-inch Hale Telescope; a marvel when it opened in 1949, it is still one of the largest in the world. The giant dome is open from 9 a.m. to 4 p.m. daily. From the viewing area, visitors can see the telescope named for George Ellery Hale, the Caltech astronomer who spearheaded the facility's construction.

Exhibits tell how the telescope was built, how it works, some of the discoveries it has produced, and a bit on the upgrades that have been made through the years. Down the hill is a gift shop (open only on weekends, except during the summer) and photos taken from the telescope. A video (apparently produced in the late 1970s) explains how it all works.

THERE ARE THREE other telescopes on the mountain: the 48-inch Oschin, the 18-inch Schmidt, and the 60-inch reflecting. Astronomers from Caltech and Cornell universities, the Carnegie Institute of Washington, and Pasadena's Jet Propulsion Laboratory use the facilities.

When construction started on the dome in 1936, all the workers and materials used Nate Harrison Grade, then and now a dirt road, to get to the top of the hill. The fully paved road, South Grade (also known as "Highway to the Stars"), wasn't completed until it was time to haul the 200-inch mirror up the hill in 1947. Work continued until January 1949, when the telescope was used for the first time.

Hiking trail at Wilderness Gardens Preserve.

Lack of pavement makes Nate Harrison Grade challenging.

Roads to Mt. Palomar

DRIVERS HAVE THEIR choice of three routes to the top of Mount Palomar: mostly unpaved Nate Harrison Grade Road on the west; South Grade near the junction with Valley Center Road; and East Grade near Lake Henshaw. All three converge at the top where a small market and restaurant are located, at Canfield Road.

Which road is best? Explore them and make up your own mind. Take one up, then another down. Just make sure you note sunset in your plans for the day and hit the road long before dark. If you think these twists and turns are a challenge to drive during the day, just try them after dark.

NATE HARRISON GRADE: If you're up for a little dirt-roading, continue from Wilderness Gardens east on SR-76 just over three miles (about 12.5 miles from I-15) to the left turn for Nate Harrison Grade Road. Named for the former slave—a resident of the mountain from the mid-late 1860s until his death in 1920—who reportedly used hand tools to create a grade wide enough for horses and wagons. An interesting article from 1958 in the Journal of San Diego described him as "Palomar's Friendly Hermit."

The road starts out meandering through orange groves, with their spectacular aroma. As the groves give way, so does most of the pavement. This is a county road but it can be rocky and rutted. More than half the road is completely dirt, which can be a mess. There are stretches with thin pavement, but that seems to only protect the areas in-between the potholes, while other areas have a loose covering of gravel. In any event, your vehicle should have plenty of ground clearance and at least all-wheel drive.

There isn't much traffic, so drivers can enjoy a slower pace and

Small store and restaurant are where all routes meet.

the challenge of avoiding ruts and rocks. There are a few turnouts to pause and enjoy the spectacular view of the beautiful Pauma Valley. Passengers, even kids, will be paying attention because of the bumps and lumps, plus the tension of sometimes having sheer cliffs right outside their window. It makes for a memorable day.

No matter your experience level, Nate Harrison Grade is a heart-pounding thrill. You're on a narrow, single-lane dirt trail with vertical cliffs on either side: one goes up, the other goes down. Not much space for mistakes. There are locals, regulars, and motorcyclists that might know the trail better than you, or may just be driving faster than your comfort level—let them pass.

A small stone monument (its plaque was missing during my last trip) marks the location of Nate Harrison's house. He supposedly put a coffee can outside the house for tolls; if it had still been there, I'd have dropped a quarter in it in Nate's memory.

It's about nine twisting miles up the hill to Palomar Mountain State Park, which you'll continue through to join county Highway S-7. A left at the junction with South Grade Road (S-6) and East Grade Road (S-7) takes you to the observatory on Canfield Road.

SOUTH GRADE: If you're not up for dirt, continue eight miles east of Nate Harrison Grade to South Grade Road, Highway S-6, also known as "The Highway to the Stars." South Grade Road was paved after World War II so the 200-inch mirror for the Palomar Observatory could be trucked up the mountain.

The trip up South Grade is shorter and more twisting than the other two, as it sort of goes straight up the mountain, at least as the crow flies. Turnouts provide vistas of the valley below.

EAST GRADE: Stay on SR-76 about another ten miles past South Grade to S-7, just before Lake Henshaw (watch out… the Palomar Mountain directional sign is on the wrong side of the intersection) to take this, the longer of the two paved routes to the top. I have an old county map from 1923, the "absolutely reliable" Thurston, which identified this as a wagon road leading up to a spot called "Nellie," near the peak of Palomar Mountain. Today, S-7 is a nice, twisting but narrow road that quickly climbs along the edge of the mountains surrounding Palomar. Views to the east are of Lake Henshaw, and Pauma Valley to the west. During the spring, flowers in bloom include wild lilac and the California poppy. Higher up, oaks and conifers shade the road.

What makes this route intimidating is its traffic—not heavy by any means, but composed of touring and sport motorcycle riders who sometimes tear around curves at angles and speeds that appear to defy gravity. Even to someone who's been driving a sports car for years, these folks can be a bit unnerving. I keep a close watch on the rear-view mirror, turn down the sound system a bit, listen for the whine of a sports bike or roar of a v-twin, and pull over when possible to let them pass.

THE OBSERVATORY: At the top of the mountain, follow Canfield Road to the Observatory. Looking at the dome is impressive enough, but what summed it all up was the "wow!" I once heard from a family as they climbed to the top of the viewing area and saw the giant telescope for the first time.

The mountain is still pretty remote. At the top of South Grade is

Observatory is a short walk from parking lot.

a small store and Mother's Kitchen Restaurant, where I've stopped and lunched on occasion. During one visit, an impromptu motorcycle show was in progress that included several sport bikes, with the (mostly) guys checking out the collection of Hondas, Yamahas, Suzukis, a few custom creations, a couple of sport tourers, and a Harley or two.

This drive has something for everybody. Country air and learning for the kids, a nice day for adults, and as challenging a drive as you want.

Take the Trip

DISTANCE: About 34 miles from I-15 to Palomar Observatory, 70 miles round trip via South Grade Road. Additional mileage using East Grade Road; additional time via Nate Harrison Grade.

DIFFICULTY: Challenging. All-wheel or four-wheel-drive vehicles recommended for unpaved Nate Harrison Grade. Twists and curves along entire route.

DIRECTIONS
- *See Google Map at goo.gl/GXb7Ox*
- Interstate 15 to SR-76, Pala Road. Head east.
- All three routes lead to Canfield Road intersection. Observatory is at the north end of Canfield Road.

ROUTE CHOICES
- **NATE HARRISON GRADE**: Left from SR-76. Continue through state park. Left at Canfield Road to observatory. To take this route from the top from Canfield Road, right at S-7,

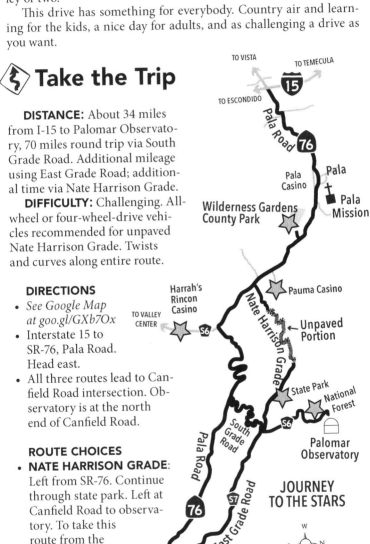

continue through state park.

- **SOUTH GRADE (S-6)**: Follow SR-76 to signs for Palomar Mountain and South Grade. Continue straight through intersection at the top onto Canfield Road and observatory.
- **EAST GRADE ROAD (S-7)**: Follow SR-76 east to just before Lake Henshaw. To return, head east from junction at the top of the mountain.

 For Nature Lovers

- About the only conifer forests left in San Diego County.
- Dirt-road driving experience.
- State Park and National Forest lands have hiking trails and campgrounds.

 Stuff for Kids

- History and old California culture at Pala Mission.
- Hiking and open space at Wilderness Gardens Preserve.
- Orange groves and dirt road fun on Nate Harrison Grade.
- Exploring Palomar Observatory.
- Mountain air, camping, and picnic areas on Palomar Mountain.

Road ends at 5,500 feet.

- School camp located in State Park might bring back memories.

 Stuff for Adults

- Good eats in Pala.
- Casinos in Pala, Pauma, and nearby Valley Center.
- Fun driving on dirt and twisting roads.
- Fresh fruit and vegetable stands along Pala Road.
- Palomar Observatory has historic and scientific exhibits.
- Palomar Mountain is a great, romantic getaway.

Old store in Pala.

💡 Sites and Eats

- *Find links to these web sources online at* www.joyride.guru/booklinks
- Wilderness Gardens Preserve
- Wilderness Gardens Feature, *San Diego Union-Tribune*
- Nate Harrison, *Journal of San Diego History*, January 1958
- Palomar Observatory
- Palomar Mountain State Park
- Palomar Star Parties, Cleveland National Forest
- Mother's Kitchen

On a late afternoon, riders head south on Sunrise Highway.

Spectacular Sunrise

SAN DIEGO COUNTY'S ONLY NATIONAL FOREST SCENIC BYWAY, SUNRISE HIGHWAY CRUISES THROUGH FOREST AND MEADOWS AT 6,000 FEET

Your Journey

WHAT'S SO GREAT about Sunrise Highway?

- It's easy to get to. Drive east on Interstate 8 to the Sunrise Highway exit, about 40 minutes (47 miles) east of central San Diego.
- It's easy to drive. While there are a few hairpin turns at the south end, most of the road has gentle curves.
- Trees. There are groves of pines and other traditional forest trees. The timber line here is about 5,000 feet.

Along Sunrise Highway.

- Food stops nearby or on the road. The restaurants in the small Mount Laguna community are open on weekends or odd hours, there's Pine Valley at the start and Julian or Cuyamaca at the end. Or take your picnic lunch and stop at one of a half-dozen picnic areas.
- It's not crowded (except when there's snow). Even on a holiday weekend, cars, motorcycles, and bicycles can be few and far-between.
- Spectacular vistas. The desert views are dramatic, as is the 5,000-foot drop. Hiking trails lead to places with ocean views.

SUNRISE HIGHWAY IS a 26-mile route from Interstate 8 at the south end to Highway 79 (Cuyamaca Highway) at the north. Much of it runs along the spine of the Laguna Mountains, the range that defines the southeastern edge central part of San Diego County.

The sheer drop-off of the mountain peaks above the desert makes for dramatic scenery. The Laguna Mountain Lodge and Store boasts it's at 6,000 feet; nearby Cuyamaca Peak, at 6,512, is the second-highest peak in San Diego County.

Out west, 6,512 feet is only moderately tall; just about 300 miles north of Cuyamaca Peak is the tallest mountain in the Lower 48, 14,494-foot Mt. Whitney. In the East, the tallest is North Carolina's Mt. Mitchell, at 6,684.

Several spots along Sunrise Highway feature views into the desert. From Kwaaymii Point (elevation 5,483 feet) near the north end of Sunrise Highway, an old road alignment overlooks the area around Agua Caliente County Park, elevation 1,350 feet. As a crow flies (or falls), it's 10 miles down; if you want to drive, it's about 47 miles via Julian. Watch your footing on the edge of the vista point.

Ask at the visitor center where you can hike to see the ocean. Yes, the ocean, about 55 miles west, is visible from on clear days.

National Byway

KNOWN LOCALLY AS A beautiful road since the advent of the automobile, Sunrise Highway has been designated a National Forest Scenic Byway since much of it runs through the Cleveland National Forest.

Historic Laguna Mountain Lodge and Store

San Diego County's only National Forest Scenic Byway, the designation highlights the driving experience through the National Forest lands. The Sunrise Byway website has suggested stopping points; here's my take on some of the sites.

- **PINE VALLEY OVERLOOK:** Just about four miles from Interstate 8, the road widens out at what's left of a gravel pit used to rebuild the road in 1937. From here, there's a vista of the town of Pine Valley and points west. In the winter, this spot is sometimes used as a tire-chain checkpoint. The old pavement is still visible on the east side of the road.

- **MEADOW INFORMATION STATION:** About 4 miles north, there's a spot where displays orient visitors to the

Pines cast shadow on Scenic Byway sign.

Laguna Mountain Recreation Area, with a map and usage rules.

- **MOUNT LAGUNA COMMUNITY, VISITOR CENTER:** A couple of restaurants (open weekends and other random hours), the Laguna Mountain Lodge and Store, a post office (zip 91948), and the area's visitor center make up the small Mount Laguna community. The visitor center is staffed by volunteers from the Laguna Mountain Volunteer Association. Public restrooms are adjacent to the visitor center.

- **KWAAYMII POINT:** Once the route of Sunrise Highway, this old road cut and parking area have a spectacular view of Agua Caliente County Park, in the desert about 4,000 feet below. An unofficial memorial area is where relatives and friends of motorcycle riders and others have posted plaques to their lost comrades.

- **THE DESERT CONNECTION** continues at the north end of Sunrise Highway. Portions are in Anza-Borrego Desert State Park; no, you're not in the desert but over the years this huge state park has added land and grown up the side of the mountains.

Picnic Perfect

THE AREA AROUND Mount Laguna is one of my favorite pack-a-lunch places, with beautiful and unique picnic areas all along Sunrise Highway. After all, where else can you eat lunch while looking at a vista that drops 4,000 feet to the desert floor?

Plan ahead if you want to picnic. The best place to pick up a picnic lunch is in Alpine, which Interstate 8 passes as it heads east. A large grocery store and several stand-alone sandwich shops are in the community, as well as that San Diego tradition, a deli in a liquor store. I usually pop into Alpine Frontier Liquor, just off the freeway at the (aptly named) Tavern Road exit, and pick up a sandwich and supplies. There's also fast food spots in Alpine (and Frosty Burger in Pine Valley), but your hot food won't be hot by the time you get to the picnic area.

Several National Forest picnic areas are right off the road, with paved access and parking. One of my favorite is the Desert View Picnic Area, with a view stretching to the Salton Sea (elevation -226.4), so you're actually looking down 6,000 feet.

There are also well-marked, unpaved driving trails all around the National Forest where you can pull off, drive a bit, and just have your picnic. No tables here, just the wilderness. Los Huecos Road runs west from the visitor center. An easy-to-drive dirt trail, it's generally

Roughing it in the Cleveland National Forest.

View from Kwaaymii Point of Agua Caliente County Park area, 4,000 feet below.

well maintained, but dirt roads can get rutty, muddy, and rocky depending on the recent weather and when it was last scraped. A passenger car might be able to take it, but it's better if your ride is an SUV.

A mile south of the settlement is Thing Valley Road, which has a name that just needs exploring. It's named for the Thing family, early settlers whose descendants still own property in the area. Gates on the trail might be closed; on one visit I was able to go a couple of miles in.

The narrow, rutted, rocky road winds through a beautiful forest, needing something with high ground clearance and all-wheel-drive just to make sure you can get in and out. Checking the altimeter, the high point along my drive was 6,040 feet. The road is generally on GPS maps, so just set your navigation system for Thing Valley Road and follow the directions.

If you can make it to Quail Springs Meadow, you'll experience a beautiful open space surrounded by hills. There are a few cabins in the area and it's generally patrolled by a park ranger.

Fee Areas

ANYTHING OFF THE highway generally requires a National Forest Adventure Pass, which is available at stores in the area, including the Laguna Mountain Lodge and Store, as well as the visitor center. At this writing, it's $5 a day, per car with four people. An annual pass is $30. Campgrounds are extra, and some hiking areas need special permits.

The National Forest parking areas are easy to spot; they generally have National Forest signs at the entry, as well as notices saying that it's a fee area. Parking along Sunrise Highway is mostly non-existent.

Hiking and Horses

SUNRISE HIGHWAY GENERALLY parallels the Pacific Crest Trail, which runs border-to-border from Mexico to Canada. If you want to experience a section of its 2,663 miles, find it at the Kwaaymii Point parking area. Shorter trails radiate out from most of the picnic and camp grounds.

Horses are allowed on many of the trails and several parking areas include room for trailers and staging. Check at the visitor center for locations and availability.

Snow, Rain, Floods and Fires

DESPITE SAN DIEGO'S reputation for mild weather, things can get rough on Mount Laguna. It experiences all four seasons, plus that wilderness specialty: brush-fire season. Scars from brush fires are evident all along the route, especially in the northern part of Sunrise Highway.

Old highway alignment is now part of Pacific Crest Trail.

Cruising on Sunrise Highway.

Burnt tree trunks from the 2003 blaze dot the hillsides, but visitors can see how the forest comes back. (This was the Cedar Fire that burned much of the Cuyamaca Rancho State Park, just west of the National Forest lands.)

Snow is also a regular visitor to Mt. Laguna, as early as November and as late as May. It melts in a few days, so there's no permanent ski area this far south. This is a fairly remote area and when a blizzard hits it can be as serious as if it's in Minnesota. Visitors are advised to be prepared when there is a snow forecast, including having tire chains.

It's a San Diego tradition to head up to the mountains when there's snow. Traffic can be horrible, as folks not accustomed to driving on ice and tire chains can go crazy.

Rainstorms and wind can also be severe even in the summer, when thunderstorms can drop an inch of rain in a short time.

Going Elsewhere

SUNRISE HIGHWAY ENDS at Highway 79, the Cuyamaca Highway, about 26 miles north of its start at Interstate 8. From there, a return to I-8 is south over Highway 79, a very twisty road through Cuyamaca. North is the mountain gold-rush town of Julian, and a long drive down Highway 78 through Ramona to Escondido, or via Highway 67 to I-8 in El Cajon. Another option is Highway 79 through Pala to Interstate 15.

Or, do what I did: Use the pullout just south of Highway 79 to make a u-turn and head back south for another enjoyable run on Sunrise Highway. Of the 150 or so National Forest Scenic Byways around the country, this is the only one in my backyard.

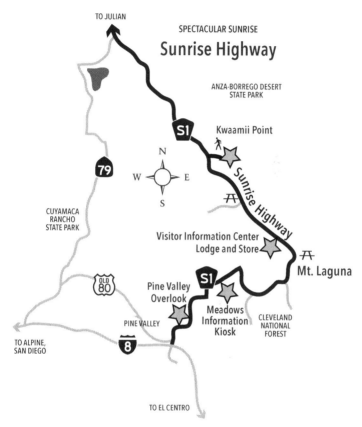

⚡ Take the Trip

DISTANCE: 26 miles from Interstate 8 to Highway 79. Exit from Interstate 8 is about 47 miles east of central San Diego.

DIFFICULTY: Easy. A few hairpins along the way, but it's mostly gentle curves.

Winter snow on Sunrise Highway.

Courtesy Laguna Mountain Lodge and Store

DIRECTIONS
See Google Map: https://goo.gl/ZjEaMJ
- Interstate 8 east to Sunrise Highway exit.
- Go north, following signs for county Highway S1, Mount Laguna and Laguna Mountain Recreation Area; that's Sunrise Highway.
- Sunrise Highway ends at Highway 79.

For Nature Lovers
- Traditional mountain flora and fauna.
- Fresh air at 6,000 feet.
- Snow in the winter.
- Hiking trails from a few feet to 2,663 miles.
- Picnic and campgrounds.

Sites and Eats
- *Find links to these web sources online at* www.joyride.guru/booklinks
- Sunrise Scenic Byway website from US Forest Service.
- Laguna Mountain Recreation Area from the US Forest Service.
- Desert View Picnic Area from the US Forest Service.
- Pacific Crest Trail from the US Forest Service.
- Agua Caliente County Park, in the Anza Borrego Desert State Park.
- Laguna Mountain Lodge and Store

Main Street in Julian.

Jaunt
to Julian

MOUNTAINS, PIE, GREAT ROADS; WHAT ELSE DO YOU NEED?

The classic San Diego day trip is a drive to Julian, elevation 4,200 feet. Generations have enjoyed this former gold-mining town's old-time charm and character, as well as its apple pie. The area also has some of the most enjoyable roads in the region.

 Your Journey

JULIAN, PIE.

To a San Diego local, those two words inspire images of a trip to the mountains—a charming town, twisting roads, apple pie, occasional snow, and a lot of smiles.

The historic mining town, dating back to the 1850s, is as well known locally as the world-famous San Diego Zoo. It's one of those places visited by natives and newcomers alike.

While the beach and bay might be the way the world sees San Diego, part of its self-image is this town of about 1,500 people at 4,200 feet in the Laguna Mountains, just over an hour's drive from central San Diego. If you haven't been there, you can't call yourself a San Diegan; it's the classic San Diego day trip.

The Town

LOOKING MORE LIKE a small town in the Sierras than Southern California, Julian has a great wild-west feel and charm, with cafés, shops and the all-important pie. Officially designated a historic district, it's unlike anything else in San Diego County. I try for a weekday visit, when it can be delightfully uncrowded even during the height of summer. If you're there on a busy day, I'd suggest ditching the car at one of the pay parking lots, located on A Street, or at 4th and B streets.

Folks will drive up the mountain just for a slice of apple pie, which is the town's unofficial dish. When settlers first arrived after the Civil War (and the town's namesake, Mike Julian, was one of them), they found that apple trees could grow here because of the town's altitude and cold winters. Julian generally gets several snowfalls every year and apple trees need some cold weather to produce fruit in volume.

The apples lead to local cafés putting apple pie on the menu and today pie is probably the biggest industry in town. Busy days will find tourists lined up for their slice, going home with pies to go and jugs of (non alcoholic) cider and juice. The pies are generally made locally (ask to make sure), as is the cider; there's nothing like the fresh stuff and believe me, it's worth the trip. There's the Julian Pie Company, Mom's Pies, Julian Café pies—you name it, they serve apple pie, ar-

Busy day in downtown Julian.

guing about whose is the best and who made the first.

The gold-rush heritage dates back to 1869, when the shiny stuff was discovered by former slave Fred Coleman. While gold production petered out by 1880, the Eagle and High Peak Mine is still around, a privately owned piece of history. A small sign points visitors there from Main and C streets, but it's a bit too far to walk.

There's also fun for the kids with gold panning and a tour at the Smith Ranch's Julian Train and Gold Mine Tour, which is a bit north of town, off of Banner Road on Ethelwyn Lane. There's gold panning, a mine, and a small train takes visitors around the property.

The town's storefronts and covered sidewalks date back, in some spots, to the gold-rush days, as does the Julian Hotel, opened and operated for years by Albert and Margaret Robinson, pioneering African Americans. Freed slave Albert found his way to the mountain community, where he met and married Margaret. Together they founded first a restaurant, then the Hotel Robinson, now known as the Julian Gold Rush Hotel. Albert died in 1915; Margaret ran the hotel until 1921. Other small hotels, bed-and-breakfast inns, and private homes and cabins are available for overnight stays. It's a wonderful getaway.

Area Roads, Parks and Hikes

Julian sits in one of a collection of canyons and ravines in the area around 5,709-foot Volcan Mountain. Farming is still big business here and the old wagon roads make for fun driving. San Diego's mountains are smaller than the Sierras or other ranges in the state, but they are just as rugged.

WYNOLA ROAD: Creating a twisting bypass of Julian, Wynola Road runs from the settlement of the same name just southwest of town to near the top of Banner Grade northeast of Julian. It curves through beautiful valleys and ravines, grazing lands, vineyards, and apple orchards. It's a spectacular few miles through a truly unique part of Southern California.

Wynola Road ends at Banner Road, after crossing a small bridge over Banner Creek. Normally calm and quaint, Banner Creek can become a raging river during rainy weather. There was once a town of Banner further down the mountain, but it was washed out during a 19th century storm (the current store and campground mark the town's former location).

FARMER ROAD: Bisecting Wynola Road is the disjointed Farmer Road, which can also be taken from downtown Julian. You'll notice that highways 78/79 make a right turn onto Main Street in Julian; the left turn takes you on Farmer Road, which curves northwest through

Today's Julian Gold Rush Hotel was built by African-Americans.

the countryside. At Wynola Road, make a right, then a quick left to stay on Farmer Road where, in addition to more great driving, you'll pass two hiking trailheads: Volcan Mountain and Santa Ysabel Preserve's Kanaka Loop Trail.

Volcan Mountain Trail is named for the highest peak in the area; its loop trail runs for more than four miles through conifer forests. Vistas of the desert and ocean, the 2,900-acre open space, and a top elevation of 5,353 feet are highlights. The park's website has more details and information on hikes lead by rangers. Park on Farmer Road.

Kanaka Loop Trail curves through the eastern part of the 3,800-acre preserve that stretches to its namesake town of Santa Ysabel. Native grasslands, oaks, and wildflowers abound in the 3,800-acre open space. The ambitious can be dropped off at the Farmer Road parking lot, then pick them up at the other end of a nearly 10 mile hike to the town of Santa Ysabel.

PINE HILLS, HEISE PARK: A bit southwest of town, follow the signs to Pine Hills, a settlement and lodge that dates from 1912. The Pine Hills Lodge has rustic cabins and a restaurant; boxer Jack Dempsey trained here for a 1926 bout (he lost).

The road twists through the hills but follow the signs to the William Heise County Park, a jewel in the area with camping and picnic grounds. At 4,200 feet, the park has forests of oak, cedar, and pines. The county has built campsites, small cabins, and camper hookups for overnighters, plus picnic areas and kids play areas for day users.

Snow

DID YOU READ THAT correctly? Snow in San Diego?

Yes, Julian and the other mountain areas in the county get several snow storms every year. There's a crush of cars and people who head to up to Julian, Santa Ysabel and Cuyamaca. Some tips:

- Leave early in the day. Traffic can be a bear.
- Carry tire chains and know how to install them. The authorities will probably require chains.
- Park in legal areas, play in public areas. Most of the fields and pastures you'll see are private property. A good way to figure that out is to look for No Trespassing signs and fences; if you see either, choose another spot. Your best bets: have fun in Julian or head to William Heise Park.
- Drive carefully. You know how to drive in snow and ice conditions, but others around you may be driving in the cold for the first time.

Check the County of San Diego website for any updates on snow conditions.

Getting There and Back

JULIAN IS ON state Highways 78/79, about an hour northeast of central San Diego. The conventional way to get there is Interstate 15 to Scripps Poway Parkway, east to state Highway 67 to Ramona, then northeast on Highway 78 (through Ramona) to town.

From San Diego's North County, take Highway 78 east until you reach town; drivers can also follow state Highway 76 (Pala Road) to Highway 79 south (it joins up with 78 in the town of Santa Ysabel),

Kanaka Trailhead just north of Julian.

then east to Julian. Another favored route from I-15 is to follow the signs to the San Diego Zoo Safari Park at Bear Valley Parkway northeast, joining Highway 78 near the park.

From El Cajon and eastern San Diego, take Highway 67 to Ramona, meeting Highway 78 in Ramona.

All roads lead to Ramona, except for the Highway 76 alternative, which means there can be a bit of traffic on twisting, single-lane Highway 78. I like to mix things up by taking an even more twisting, but generally less crowded alternative, the Old Julian Highway.

Highways 78 and 79 run in tandem through the Julian area.

THE STORY GOES THAT the Old Julian Highway was the original wagon road from Julian, following the terrain and passing many of the ranches existing in the 19th century. Access it at Third Street in Ramona, where Main Street narrows and runs out of town. Watch for the left turn onto Old Julian Highway, which today is a beautiful, twisting road through the ranch lands of rural Ramona. It is narrow, with plenty of blind curves and cross streets, so be very careful, especially if you're not accustomed to country roads.

Look for the camels of the Oasis Camel Dairy just before Old Julian Highway joins Highway 78 a few miles west of the small settlement of Santa Ysabel. Yes, camels in the mountains of Southern California. The camels live on the ranch, contributing their milk for a variety of products. It's open to visitors a few weekends a year.

Make a note to stop on the way back and shop in Santa Ysabel, once a service town for watering the horses or early automobiles, now sort of a Julian suburb. There's Dudley's Bakery, a local landmark, which has been making all sorts of exotic breads and baked goodies for decades. Julian Pie Company has its commercial bakery here, where it makes pies that are sold here, at its shop in Julian, and at stores all over Southern California. And Don's Market has one of the more exotic meat counters, where you can get unique homemade sausage for tomorrow's barbecue.

From Santa Ysabel, follow Highways 78/79 northeast to town. If it's your first visit, I'd save the other drives for the route back or another day.

AND SPEAKING OF THE way back, along Highway 78 is the Pine

Hill Egg Ranch, just north of Ramona. Buy eggs fresh from the ranch at the small store. There are a few other fruit and vegetable stands along the route where you can pick up other locally grown goods.

There is no doubt that this is the classic San Diego day trip. It's a change from the beach or Balboa Park and certainly different than the big-box strip mall where most folks do their shopping. The fresh mountain air makes it seem like it's a world away, but it's not. It's right here in your hometown's back yard.

Take the Trip

• *See Google Map:* http://goo.gl/LZQRdc

VIA RAMONA

FROM INTER-STATE 15 IN SOUTH-ERN SAN DIEGO COUNTY

• Interstate 15 to Scripps Poway Parkway. Head east.
• Left at state Highway 67. Continue on Highway 67 to Ramona, joining state Highway 78 on Main Street. Continue northeast to Julian.

WYNOLA/FARMER ROAD ALTERNATIVE (ON GOOGLE MAP)

• In Wynola, left at Wynola Road.
• Right at Farmer Road. Continue onto Main Street in Julian.

FROM INTERSTATE 15 IN NORTHERN SAN DIEGO COUNTY
Route Choice 1
• Follow Highway 78 through Escondido; continue through Ramona to Julian.
Route Choice 2
• Interstate 15 to Bear Valley Parkway (follow signs to San Diego Zoo Safari Park).
• Right at San Pasqual Road.
• Right at Highway 78, San Pasqual Valley Road.

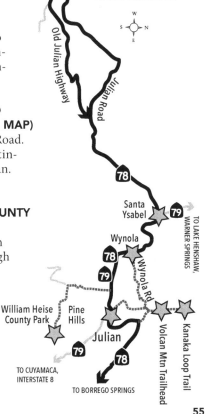

Route Choice 3
- Interstate 15 to state Highway 76 (Pala Road). East to Highway 79 (end of Highway 76).
- Right at Highway 79. Continue on Highway 79 to Julian (joins Highway 78 at Santa Ysabel).

Twisting Roads

All the routes to Julian have twists and turns; here are some fun drives in the area.

OLD JULIAN HIGHWAY: A twisty alternative from Ramona to near Santa Ysabel through farm and grazing lands.
- Right at Third Street from Highway 78 (Main Street) on the northeast side of Ramona.
- Left at Old Julian Highway.
- Right at Highway 78.

WYNOLA ROAD: Twisting farm road around ranches north of Julian.
- From Julian, continue north on Highway 78.
- Left at Wynola Road, about 2 miles east of Highway 79 and post office.
- Road ends at Highways 78/79 in Wynola. To return to Julian, left at Highways 78/79. To return to Ramona and I-15, right at Highways 78/79.

FARMER ROAD: Farmer Road is the northwest continuation of Main Street. Street name changes at A Street in Julian, one block west of Washington Street; Washington Street is where Highway 78/79 turns right onto Main Street.

🐢 For Nature Lovers
- Wonderful parks, hiking, camping in the clean mountain air.
- If you don't see wild turkeys, deer and other wildlife, you're not looking.
- Vistas of mountains, deserts, ocean (on clear days).
- Outstanding getaway from the city, only an hour's drive (give or take).

👧 Stuff for Adults
- Several wineries and even a microbrewery in Julian.
- Quaint shops with antiques and crafts.
- Love that pie.

Don't miss a stop at Dudley's Bakery in Santa Ysabel.

- Bed and breakfast inns, so make it a weekend.
- A variety of twisting, curving roads for driving fun.

☺ Stuff for Kids

- Old West fun.
- A real gold mine (or two).
- Parks and hiking.
- Camping.
- Pie.

♀ Sites and Eats

- *Find links to these web sources online at* www.joyride.guru/booklinks
- Don's Market, 30250 Highway 78, Santa Ysabel, CA 92070, (760) 765 3272. Small supermarket also has a full-service meat counter with homemade sausage, bison, elk, and venison.
- Dudley's Bakery, 30218 Highway 78, Santa Ysabel, CA 92070, (760) 765-0488. Closed Tuesday and Wednesday. Founded by Dudley Pratt in 1963, current owner Barry Brunye carries on the tradition of this big, neighborhood-style bakery in an unlikely location. Worth a visit; closed Tuesday-Wednesday.
- Eagle and High Peak Mine, 2320 C Street, Julian, CA 92036, (442) 777-8646. Hard-rock mining tunnels have been restored to their 1880s look. Take a one-hour guided tour.
- William Heise County Park, 4945 Heise Park Road, Julian, CA 92036, (760) 765-0650. County of San Diego park open for day use

and camping. Trees keep things cool in the summer, snow falls in the winter. Great for day use, with kids play areas and picnic tables. Overnight use available, with campsites, trailers hookups; one of the few county parks with cabins.

- Julian Gold Rush Hotel, 2032 Main Street P.O. Box 1856, Julian, CA 92036, (760) 765-0201. Historic hotel dates to 1890s.
- Julian Pie Company, 21976 Hwy. 79, Santa Ysabel, CA 92070, (760) 765-2400; 2225 Main Street, Julian, CA 92036, (760) 765-2449. Since 1984, the Smothers family has run the pie business and a Julian-area orchard. If the Julian shop is too crowded, stop in at Santa Ysabel on the way home.
- Julian Train and Gold Mine Tour, "next to" 2353 Ethelyn Lane, Julian, CA 92036, (760) 765-2288. Ride a hand-pushed 1898-vintage mine car, ride a train around the property and explore the mine, dug in the 1870s.
- Kanaka Trail, Santa Ysabel Preserve, Santa Ysabel East Staging Area, 500 Farmer Road, Julian, CA 92036, (760) 765-4098 or (760) 814-0208. County of San Diego 3,800-acre open space preserve has more than 13 miles of trails for hiking, biking, and horseback riding from Farmer Road parking lot.
- Mom's Pies, 2119 Main St., Julian, CA 92036, 4510 Highway 78 (Wynola), (760) 765-2264. Baking since 1984, Mom (Anita Nichols) is one of the town favorites. If the line is too long in town, stop by the Wynola location on your way home.
- Oasis Camel Dairy, 26757 Highway 78, Ramona, CA 92065, (760) 787-0983. Ranch raises and cares for camels, producing camel-milk soap. Open a few days a year for public tours and events.
- Pine Hill Egg Ranch, 25818 Highway 78, Ramona, CA 92065, (760) 789-0195. Local egg ranch has a small retail counter just off the highway. A carton of farm-fresh eggs is worth the stop; large quantities available for that really big baking project.
- Pine Hills Lodge, 2960 La Posada Way Julian, CA 92036, (760) 765-1100. "Above the clouds, among the gigantic pines of the Cuyamaca Mountain, elevation 4,316 feet" reads the cover of a 1920s brochure for this historic lodge.
- Snow in the mountains. From as early as November to as late as May, there can be snowfalls in the Julian area. Check the County of San Diego website for any information, or its road closures and traffic conditions page.
- Volcan Mountain Preserve, 1209 Farmer Road/Wynola Road, Julian, CA 92036, (760) 765-4098 or (760) 814-0208. County of San Diego 2,900-acre preserve with 5-mile hiking trail. Closed during and after half-inch or more of rain or any snow. Park on Farmer Road.

Along Boulder Creek Road.

Curves, Dirt and Cuyamaca

BOULDER CREEK ROAD TO CUYAMACA HIGHWAY JOURNEY IS CHALLENGING, BEAUTIFUL

Enjoy a 45-mile loop in the central portion of the Laguna Mountains in eastern San Diego County through natural open space and Cuyamaca Rancho State Park. Includes challenging curves on SR-79 through Cuyamaca, 18 miles of public, un-paved road; all-wheel drive or 4-wheel drive recommended. It's a must for anyone who lives in San Diego.

Vista along Boulder Creek Road.

⬡ Your Journey

CALL THIS ONE a hidden treasure cruise.

Not only is the road we're taking one of the beauties in San Diego County, but it utilizes something that the thousands of folks who own all-wheel drive cars, trucks and SUVs rarely use: the vehicle's capabilities on dirt roads.

Most drivers heading to the mountain town of Julian or Cuyamaca take SR-78 through Ramona, or SR-79 from Descanso to the south. Sure, there are variants using Sunrise Highway through Mt. Laguna, or Old Julian Highway north from Ramona, but drivers use the routes they know.

There are other ways. If your car has all-wheel drive, why not give it a little exercise on a public, unpaved road? Boulder Creek Road is a perfect spot to see a little of what makes AWD them so popular in snow country and with rally drivers around the world.

Running between Descanso, which means "rest" in Spanish, and the Julian suburb of Pine Hills, is about 18 miles of mostly graded dirt; a portion of the more than 100 miles of public, unpaved roads in San Diego County. If you've only experienced urban Southern California, here's a real treat. Boulder Creek dissects a wilderness area that's mostly covered with our native chaparral, including the distinctive red-trunked manzanita. A favorite with birders and hikers, this byway is a look back to the region's past.

After leaving civilization in Descanso, our trail clings to the rugged, chaparral-covered hills. Native oaks provide a cooling canopy in spots as the byway swings near Boulder Creek and other water sources. It ends at Pine Hills, where our route turns east over twisty, but paved Engineers Road to SR-79, then south by Lake Cuyamaca and through Cuyamaca Rancho State Park, back to Descanso and the freeway.

BEGIN YOUR DRIVE by exiting Interstate 8 at the Descanso/SR-79 offramp, which is east of El Cajon and Alpine if you're coming from San Diego, and west of Pine Valley if you're coming from the desert. Head north into the small mountain town of Descanso, a quaint little settlement nestled into the peaks and valleys. What most people think of as Descanso, located at the intersection of SR-79 and Riverside Drive, is actually Descanso Junction. This collection of small commercial buildings dates back to before World War II, when the main highway from San Diego to the east, US 80, was realigned; it's now been designated "Historic Old Highway 80."

We're heading up Riverside Drive, bridging the Sweetwater River and turning at the long-established Perkins Market (since 1875). This is the original route east, up Viejas Grade from the west, around the Sweetwater River and joining the 1920s alignment of Old Highway 80 near the current intersection with SR-79.

Fording a stream near Inaja Indian Reservation.

From the store, take Oak Grove Drive to Boulder Creek Road. As what passes for civilization in Descanso fades out, so does the pavement. For the next 18 miles or so, it's mostly wide, twisty light gravel, with a few ruts. The County tries to get out and grade them twice a year, so unless we've had a good rain the roads are fine even for standard sedans.

For an all-wheel drive vehicle, this is perfect. A little speed (we're talking 25 mph) and a few controlled slides around the corners add just a bit more fun to the spectacular view. Much of this road is through the coast range of Southern California in its natural state. The rolling hills, rugged canyons, rocks, and the brownish green of native chaparral are a feast for the eyes, even in a drought year. Boulder Creek Road passes near the ignition point of the devastating 2003 Cedar Fire, which burned as far west as MCAS Miramar and east into Cuyamaca Rancho State Park.

Most likely, this road was cut through sometime around the 1869-70 Julian gold rush, when the town developed, providing an alternative to the routes still used today to Escondido.

AT TIMES, THE UNPAVED ROAD hugs the hills, rising and falling over the rugged terrain. For much of the drive, you'll most likely be all alone in nature. Homes are few and far-between, providing city-dwellers with an undisturbed wilderness view an hour or so from home.

There's a busy spot at the access to the Three Sisters Trail, a popular hiking spot with a waterfall. When I visited, cars were parked on both sides of the road. It seems like hanging out at a waterfall

Take it easy for easy driving on the unpaved Boulder Creek Road.

in arid San Diego County would be a fun way to spend a day, but a few miles up the road, an ambulance tore down the dirt road, probably headed to the falls where it seems injuries are a regular event.

To the north is the Inaja Indian Reservation (no casino, services or anything else for visitors here), before ending at the Pine Creek fire station.

Instead of heading through Pine Hills to SR-78 and Julian, I opted to take the twisty and

No services here.

paved Engineer Road east to Lake Cuyamaca, a small, man-made reservoir dating back more than a century. Local booster Ed Fletcher built the road to connect his Pine Hills development to the lake, which he had built to provide water. The road was named for Army engineers who worked on it about a century ago.

There's a store and a restaurant on the southwest side of the lake; purchase admission here if you want to fish, boat, or use the picnic areas. It's a different pass than the one required to hike and use the facilities in the state park, just to the south. Highway 79, Cuyamaca Highway, is beautiful and challenging, certainly on any local's list of roads to drive.

AND YOU SHOULD have a park pass, which is on sale at the Cuyamaca store, if you're going to visit the remnants of the old Stonewall Mine, which is just southeast of the lake. There are several picnic areas, hiking trails and other attractions along the way.

I generally stop in at the park's Visitor Center, located at 13652 Highway 79. In addition to the exhibits on the area's history and always interesting conversations with the park rangers and volunteers, it's a nostalgic spot for me as it's located next to the Cuyamaca school camp, where I spent sixth-grade camp way back in 1969. The school camp has managed to survive several serious brush fires over the years; not so lucky was the adjacent Dyer House, which burned in the 2003 fire. The home of the family that once owned what's now the state park, it served as the park headquarters and visitor center for years. Restoration of the ruin hasn't happened yet.

But mostly, I love just taking the drive from the lake to Descanso, which is a mix of challenging hairpin turns and a few nice straightaways. Take it easy, as this drive can test anyone's skill, especially if you're taking an SUV for the dirt portion of this drive. Sports cars, motorcycles, and bicyclists love the highway, so be aware of the traf-

Lake Cuyamaca is a historic oasis.

fic. The loop is about 40 miles and takes most of the day, with slow driving on the unpaved sections and more than a few stops to take in the view.

Many urban Southern California drivers are paying for all-wheel drive that they hardly ever use. Here's a way to give your car some needed exercise and see some of the real beauty in our county. It's just a few minutes up the freeway from home and well worth the trip.

⚡ Take the Trip

DISTANCE: About 45 miles. Descanso/SR-79 exit from Interstate 8 is about 35 miles east of central San Diego.

DIFFICULTY: Moderate, with twisting, narrow gravel and paved highways. All-wheel or front-wheel drive with high ground clearance recommended.

DIRECTIONS

- *See Google Map:* http://goo.gl/nhdBaW
- Interstate 8 east to SR-79/Japatul Valley Road exit.
- Right on Japatul Valley Road.
- Left onto Riverside Drive.
- Left at Viejas Grade (Perkins Market).
- Quick right at Oak Grove Drive.
- Right at Boulder Creek Road.
- Right at Engineers Road.
- Right at SR-79
- Right at Old Highway 80. Follow to Interstate 8.

 # For Nature Lovers

- Drive through wilderness areas of Cleveland National Forest and Cuyamaca Rancho State Park.
- Hiking trails at several locations.
- Rugged terrain.
- Coastal and mountain ecosystems.
- Spectacular views.

Stuff for Kids

- Picnicking and boating at Lake Cuyamaca
- Horse trails in Cuyamaca Rancho State Park.
- Camping at Cuyamaca Rancho State Park.

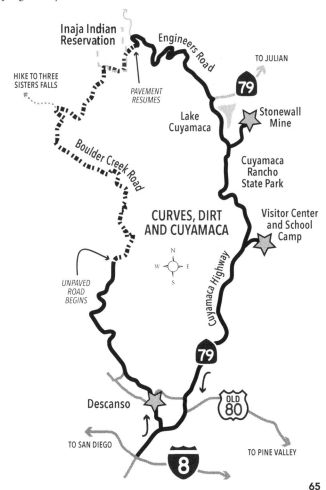

Cuyamaca is fire-scarred but still beautiful.

Sites and Eats

- *Find links to these web sources online at* www.joyride.guru/booklinks
- Descanso Junction Restaurant, 8306 Highway 79, Descanso. I stopped here for breakfast, as it was recommended by a friend as one of the better roadside cafés in the East County mountains. The breakfast wasn't the best, but my friend insists I must have caught them on a bad day.
- Pine Hills Lodge, 2960 La Posada Way, Julian. This historic lodge just outside of Julian has been around for more than a century; boxer Jack Dempsey used to train there before fights. They advertise a Sunday brunch, but I'd call ahead. The last time I was there, the restaurant and bar were closed the other six days of the week.
- Boulder Creek Road at Alltrails.com: Hikes along the road.
- Boulder Creek Road at San Diego Birding Trails: Local birding community's take on the flying residents.
- Julian Chamber of Commerce. Check for restaurants and hotels, shopping and history of this one-time booming gold rush town.
- Stonewall Mine archaeological investigation.

Riding the line on a twisting road.

Crazy Couser

SCARY CURVES MAKE INLAND NORTH COUNTY RUN ONE OF SAN DIEGO'S BEST

Twisting, curving 20-mile route parallels Interstate 15 from just outside Escondido north to Pala Road. It requires careful and attentive driving. Roads are narrow with blind driveways and hairpin curves, with frequent stretches that have little or no shoulder, as well as encroachment by everything from trees to boulders to guardrails. Views include mountains and valleys, ranches, and canopies created by adjacent trees. It's a blast for bicycle and motorcycle riders, and for drivers of modern sedans and sports cars. A bit more challenging for classic car drivers whose cars are equipped with solid rear axles (if you have one, you'll know what I'm talking about).

Narrow road with spectacular views.

🜂 Your Journey

INTERSTATE 15 NORTH OF Escondido takes a truly beautiful route through the mountains of northern San Diego County on its way to the Temecula valley. Other roads through these mountains aren't so smooth; take, for example, this route that includes the spectacular-scary Couser Canyon Road.

A few years back I visited with members of the local De Tomaso Pantera club, owner/guardians of the early 1970s Italian-American sports car that boasted a swoopy Tom Tejarda-designed body and a growling Ford V8. What was their favorite road? Without exception, they answered "Couser Canyon Road." That's where we're heading today, adding two other twisting, narrow roads to create one of the most beautiful and challenging drives in San Diego County.

These roads have what gets the blood flowing for the driving enthusiast: twists and curves, light traffic, and beautiful scenery. The route over Circle R Drive, West Lilac, Lilac, and Couser Canyon roads transitions from resort living to rural-urban to farm country over its 18 miles. The beginning and end of the route boasts spectacular vistas.

Like many old throughways in San Diego County, these byways have roots as old farm roads from the 19th or early 20th century; parts haven't been improved much since then. These curves aren't gentle—they're hairpins on top of hairpins in some spots. The route can be scarily narrow, with trees sometimes sharing the lane and... what's a shoulder? Keep alert and be sure to drive within your abilities.

I don't want to scare off mom or dad from taking this route in the minivan. A carload of kids can get a great education from this trip, and the curves might keep them looking out the window instead of at their smart phones or video games. City dwellers can't often believe that such a rural, bucolic area is minutes from home. There are also a couple of golf courses at the beginning of the route, the great Deer Park Winery and Auto Museum, plus spots to eat at the beginning and end.

THE GOOD NEWS IS that there's usually not a lot of traffic over Circle R Drive, West Lilac, Lilac, and Couser Canyon roads. Traffic is busy at the end, on Pala Road; less so over Old Highway 395/Champagne Boulevard.

Champagne Boulevard? Before I-15 opened in the early 1980s, the way north was old U.S. 395, this same stretch of tarmac. Bandleader Lawrence Welk opened his resort with a golf course, motel, and mobile home park in the 1960s. It's still there, having grown over the years.

Once the freeway was finished, this stretch of road was renamed in honor of Welk, whose face and music has been on generations of senior citizens' TVs every Saturday night since 1952. His orchestra was nicknamed the "Champagne Music Makers."

Pass the resort and you'll be at our starting point—one of the best private car spots anywhere—the Knapp family's Deer Park Winery and Auto Museum. Advertised as the "World's Largest Auto Museum of Convertibles and Americana," it has rare ragtops, memorabilia, and other eclectic collections. The museum buildings and grounds are popular gathering spots for families, car clubs, and wed-

Classic cars at Deer Park.

dings (29013 Champagne Blvd., Escondido, 760-749-1666).

The museum houses the collection of the late Robert Knapp, a Northern California winemaker who came south from Napa Valley in 1979 to found the museum. Several buildings contain rare cars (mostly convertibles), Barbies, Coca-Cola memorabilia, and early televisions, among other things. Knapp started his car collection in 1952, with a $35 1928 Ford Model A. It's now under the care of Clark Knapp, Robert's son, and is (mostly) open Friday-Sunday.

Back in 1994, the elder Knapp collaborated with local writer Dan Burger on a photo book of the collection, *They Don't Make 'Em Like That Anymore*. It's out of print, but copies are sometimes available.

From Deer Park, head north to Circle R Drive and up into the hills; this where the driving gets challenging. A racing school instructor recently described a crash as "the driver ran out of talent." Run out of talent on this drive and you could end up in a head-on collision, fly off the side of a cliff, or hit a tree.

Circle R Drive is named after the golf course and hotel development that began back in 1948. But don't look for the Circle R Resort today—it's now called the Tuscany Hills Resort and Spa, and the golf course is now part of Castle Creek Country Club. Last time I visited, the restaurant in the golf club was open to the public and had a decent cheeseburger. But I'd save my appetite for Nessy Burgers at the end of the route.

AFTER PASSING THE resort, the fun begins as Circle R Drive twists up the hillsides. Watch for the sharp right turn to West Lilac Road, the first of what are probably old farm roads. They're narrow, with ups-and-downs, sometimes banked the wrong way—they go around obstacles such as trees, boulders, and farmers' fields. The Lilac roads were named for the California Lilac, which grew natural-

Great views of San Diego's agricultural center.

Setting sun casts shadows on Couser Canyon Road.

ly in this area; there was once a town here named Lilac.

Keep super-alert through the whole drive. Mind the "twist-ing-road" signs and try to look ahead, anticipating the next obsta-cle. Any modern car or SUV can handle this easily. Owners of classic cars have to be extra careful as vintage brakes and suspension can be challenged by this type of road. Solid axles, slow steering, and drum brakes combined with too much horsepower make these roads haz-ardous without a cautious driver behind the wheel.

Bottom line: The route is worth the risk, just be careful.

The drive over the Lilacs is beautiful and very rural. Small ranch-es (with mostly Valley Center addresses) line the roads, where folks keep horses, chickens, and a few cows here and there. It's a wonderful country lifestyle if you're skilled in cleaning out stables and chicken coops. A few grow avocados, which were a big cash crop in this area in the early part of the 20th Century.

Keep a special lookout for Couser Canyon Road, on your left. If you miss the turn, you'll end up where Lilac Road turns to dirt; if you do, just turn around and go back.

NAMED FOR GEORGE COUSER—who bought the ranch in the canyon around 1900—our featured road in this drive goes around and over the hills, at times clinging to the canyon walls as it descends first into Double Canyon, then into Couser Canyon, where it meets up with Pala Road (state Route 76). More small ranches line the road, at times covered by a canopy of native oaks and other trees. On a hot day, this shade can be a delightful respite, especially if you're driving a convertible with the top down. On cool, foggy or rainy days, be careful of the damp pavement.

After finishing the twists, Couser Canyon Road straightens out as it reaches its end at SR-76. At this point, you're driving through San Diego County's breadbasket, center of the more than $4 billion agricultural economy.

After strenuous driving, there's nothing better than a burger. Our final destination is Nessy Burgers, the Pala Road/Interstate 15 roadside stand. The stand moved a bit north, adjacent to the Pala Mesa Market, but it's still as popular as when it opened in 1989.

No matter what takes you there, these three roads are among the best in the county for their beauty and challenge. Enjoy the ride.

Take the Trip

DISTANCE: About 20 miles.

DIFFICULTY: Challenging. Twisting, curving, narrow roads.

DIRECTIONS
- *See Google Map:* http://goo.gl/RzCyTl
- Interstate 15 to Deer Springs Road exit, about 30 miles north of central San Diego.
- Exit to right on Deer Springs Road
- Left onto Champagne Boulevard.
- Right at Circle R Drive
- Right at West Lilac Road.
- Left at Lilac Road.
- Left at Couser Canyon Road.
- Left at Pala Road (CA-76)
- Right at Old Highway 395. Nessy Burger is a half-mile north.

For Nature Lovers
- Sweet smells of orange groves, especially in the spring.
- Watch for the livestock checking you out along the way.
- Spotty Internet connections.
- It's just not the city.

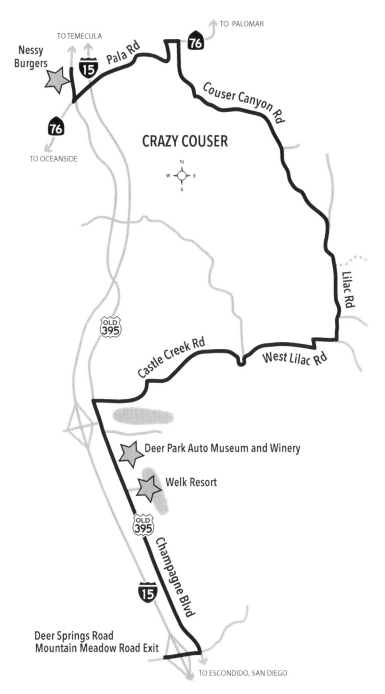

TO PALOMAR

76

Nessy Burgers

TO TEMECULA

Pala Rd

15

CRAZY COUSER

Couser Canyon Rd

76

TO OCEANSIDE

N
W E
S

Lilac Rd

OLD 395

Castle Creek Rd

West Lilac Rd

Deer Park Auto Museum and Winery

Welk Resort

OLD 395

Champagne Blvd

15

Deer Springs Road
Mountain Meadow Road Exit

TO ESCONDIDO, SAN DIEGO

Nessy Burger is a reward at the end of a challenging drive.

Stuff for Kids

- Cool cars at Deer Park Auto Museum.
- Horses, cows, and other animals at ranches along the way.
- Twisting road might make them look up from their tablet.
- What kid doesn't like a big cheeseburger?

Sites and Eats

- *Find links to these web sources online at*
  www.joyride.guru/booklinks
- Deer Park Winery and Auto Museum
- Rancho Lilac, Valley Center Historical Society
- Nessy Burger
- Welk Village Resort

Unique markers show boundary of "The Ranch."

Roads of the Ranch

EXCLUSIVE SAN DIEGO COUNTY ENCLAVE, RANCHO SANTA FE, MAKES A PERFECT DAY TRIP

Wooded, gently curving streets, and beautiful estates highlight this exclusive San Diego County community. Planned from the start to be an idealized "Old Spanish California" town, the Ranch has cool ties to old Hollywood days of Bing Crosby, Douglas Fairbanks Jr., and Victor Mature. Grab glimpses of the "one percent" at the end of long driveways, along with groves of eucalyptus and citrus, plus paddocks for the horses. Roads are easy to maneuver; the village offers restaurants and a few shops, plus banks and real-estate offices in case you want to purchase one of the eight-figure estates.

Historic buildings are in the Ranch's downtown section.

〰️ Your Journey

ONE OF THE WEALTHIEST communities in the world owes its existence to broken railroad ties, the bucolic vision of California popular in the late 19th and 20th centuries, and a pioneering woman architect and planner.

My personal introduction to the area came as a kid. Sunday drives combined our family tradition of happy wandering, with my dad's cheap streak that took us 30 miles out of our way to save a few pennies on gasoline.

Today, its wonderful rolling hills are crossed by meandering roads, great for driving to see exclusive mansions that sell for upwards of eight figures, and a village that looks like something out of a classic Hollywood Zorro movie.

The area we're talking about is Rancho Santa Fe, located east of Solana Beach in San Diego's North County. It's a place I love to visit—an Old Spanish California fantasy land, but at the same time a living, breathing community. Although many of the homes (and some of the surrounding communities) are behind gates, the roads are public. There's also the appeal of the quaint little town center in this early master-planned community.

In my travels around California, I haven't found anyplace that's more like the "Old Spanish California" glorified in books and movies: rambling ranchos on hilltops; small towns with tree-lined streets; everything with stucco walls and red-tile roofs. Whether played by Douglas Fairbanks, Tyrone Power, or Guy Williams, it was Zorro sweeping señoritas off their feet.

In reality, Southern California then was a pretty dry, dusty, flea-infested place, and the original Spanish settlers were nothing like this glorified vision, which predates Hollywood. It started with Helen Hunt Jackson's 1884 novel *Ramona*, a best-seller in its time, and was perpetuated in 1919's *Zorro*, by Johnson McCulley.

Visiting

THE RANCH, AS THE locals call it, is centrally located to the population centers of San Diego County, a place that's bigger than two states, Delaware and Rhode Island, and almost as big as Connecticut. An easy San Diego day trip, it's about a half-hour from central San Diego on the south and Oceanside on the north, less from Escondido, mostly by freeway. Because of its convenience, visitors can drop in for lunch, do some rubbernecking and be back home by dinner.

Most of San Diego's great drives aren't something that is easily, or conveniently, experienced without a car. A trip to the Ranch can be a great day via train and bus, with a minimum of hassle. Take the Coaster or Amtrak train to the Solana Beach station, then take a North County Transit bus to Rancho Santa Fe.

Via de la Valle is the classic route from Del Mar, ducking under Interstate 5 and heading over this sometimes busy, mostly two-lane country road. In the 1920s, this was the fastest way to the nearest train station, at Del Mar (the stop moved to Solana Beach in 1995). Parts of the route look much the same as they did when the development was young. In this pleasant valley, there are still a few farms, horse ranches, and open spaces along the San Dieguito River.

From the east, at Interstate 15, the drive over Del Dios Highway

Watch for the homes at the top of the hills.

The Inn at Rancho Santa Fe was built by the Santa Fe Railroad.

is just as scenic. It runs through the north edge of the Del Dios community and along the shore of Lake Hodges, a reservoir built to supply water to Rancho Santa Fe.

History

WE PICK UP OUR Rancho Santa Fe story a few years before *Zorro* was published, when the Santa Fe Railroad imported fast-growing eucalyptus trees in order to make railroad ties. The open land near San Diego was cheap and sunny—perfect for the Australian trees.

Unfortunately, when hit with railroad spikes, the eucalyptus wood would split. That left the company with 8,800 acres and a worthless grove of eucalyptus trees.

In 1921, the railroad began developing the property into the fantasy land of Ramona and Zorro, attracting some of the Hollywood elite and others looking to live their dreams. A small town was created and Rancho Santa Fe was born. Singer Bing Crosby was an early resident, as were other stars, including Victor Mature, Robert Young, and Milburn Stone. Crosby held his first "clambake" golf get-together at the local course; it evolved and moved to Pebble Beach, where it's still held.

By 1928, the railroad had sold most of the property and moved on. The Rancho Santa Fe Association was created to supervise the "covenant area" where property has all sorts of deed restrictions.

The association is still around today and supervising the community, regulating architecture, lot sizes, types of buildings, and many other aesthetics. It's a non-profit (and non-government) association that helps the Sheriff with security, keeps the streets paved, and runs the golf course.

A century after the eucalyptus-railroad-tie experiment failed, it's now a community that Zorro and Ramona might recognize, if they had an average annual income of more than $1 million (as reported for 2015). Bill Gates is among the 21st century elites that call it home, at least part time.

FOR THE REST OF US, it's a nice place to visit and home to wonderful roads. It's a low-speed cruise, great for a Sunday trip. See how the other half lives or pick up a $10 million mansion for yourself. Give the Buick or the Bentley a little exercise.

It's an enclave of civility where visitors must watch for both golf carts and horses in crosswalks. Pedestrians? Extra worries here, except in "downtown," because there aren't any sidewalks.

Today, on drives around Rancho Santa Fe, I get to use the skills honed as a kid on Sunday drives. Seated in the back of our 1964 Pontiac Catalina, I picked up viewing tips from my dad. He was able to maneuver the big Pontiac on the curving streets, while at the same time knowing how to spot a driveway or hedge gap to see the house at the end of the long drive.

Be sure to spend some time in the delightful business district at the center of the Ranch. The centerpiece of the "civic center" (now called the village) is the Inn at Rancho Santa Fe, located at the west end of the town's main street, Paseo Delicias (county S-6). Small shops, restaurants, and a plethora of banks and stock brokers fill the mostly low-rise, red-tile-roofed, California Spanish-styled commercial buildings.

Bing Crosby started his famous golf tournament at the local course.

Many of the oldest buildings, including the Inn, were designed by Lillian Rice, a pioneering San Diego architect, who was master architect for the developer. Rice worked for Requa and Jackson, the architectural firm that the Santa Fe Railroad selected to turn their worthless eucalyptus grove into a money-making residential development.

Visit the Rancho Santa Fe Historical Society for a walking tour and more history; it also organizes home tours as a fund raiser.

ROADS OF THE RANCH

 # Take the Trip

Usually, drives in the *Joyride Guru* series have links to a Google Map route. My apologies, but I just couldn't get the mapping software to work on these tight loops at the time this book was published. Check my website, www.joyride.guru/booklinks, for any update.

That doesn't mean you'll get lost.

With the variety of ways to get to the Ranch and the proliferation of GPS devices, just set your map to the Inn at Rancho Santa Fe, 5951 Linea Del Cielo, Rancho Santa Fe, CA 92067. Here are directions for the most popular ways to find Rancho Santa Fe.

FROM THE WEST AND INTERSTATE 5

CLASSIC ROUTE: Exit Interstate 5 at Via De La Valle (county Highway S-6), heading east. At Paseo Delicias, turn left and you're in the village.

QUICKEST ROUTE: Lomas Santa Fe Drive (county Highway S-2) is the most direct entry. Just head east from the freeway, following Lomas Santa Fe past the beautiful San Dieguito County Park. Just east, enter the covenant area as the road changes its name to Linea del Cielo. Continue east to the village.

FROM ENCINITAS AND THE NORTHWEST: Exit Interstate 5 at Encinitas Boulevard, then head east. Where Encinitas Boulevard meets Manchester Avenue and Rancho Santa Fe Road, keep going straight (southeast) onto South Rancho Santa Fe Road.

Cross the Escondido Creek bridge and to the border of the covenant area. Follow the traffic to the right onto La Bajada, then Los Morros and then along the golf course via La Granada, and into the village.

FROM THE EAST, INTERSTATE 15: Exit at Via Rancho Parkway, heading west to Del Dios Highway (S-6). Go left (south) on Del Dios Highway; the Ranch is about 10 minutes (depending on traffic) away. Go straight onto Paseo Delicias into downtown.

PUBLIC TRANSIT: Yes, you can get to this rural area on public transit, which means someone else does the driving on your joyride. If you're visiting San Diego without a car, here's a way to discover something other than the traditional tourist destinations.

Catch Amtrak or the Coaster to the Solana Beach station, then take the North County Transit bus route 308 to the town center. The bus winds through the Ranch over Via de

Original block in Rancho Santa Fe.

la Valle, giving you a brief look at some of the mansions on the south part of the covenant zone. After this taste of the Ranch, spend a few hours wandering around the village, then return home without having to fight traffic.

Driving Around the Ranch

A GENTLEMAN BY THE name of W. E. Hodges (yes, the lake was named for him) headed up the development of the Ranch for the railroad. His engineer, L.G. Sinnard, is credited with creating the meandering roads and estate-sized lots that emphasized views and country charm.

The Ranch isn't a big places, so the following routes will take you around Sinnard's roads in a few minutes. My favorite thing is to just start driving and making turns as they come up. The Ranch is not a very big place and if you get lost, just set your GPS for Del Mar, Solana Beach, or Escondido and it will get you home.

Ranch Routes

SOUTHWEST CORNER: This loop that will take you from the village, along the golf course, and down some of the residential streets.
- **START:** Paseo Delicias and La Granada.
- North on La Granada (county S-9). Follow Rancho Santa Fe Golf Course.
- Left on Ramblas de las Flores.
- Left at El Secreto.
- Left at Avenida Maravillas.
- Right at La Granada to return to village.

Classic El Camino Real bell.

NORTHERN LOOP: The terrain is less hilly on the northern part of the covenant area. Owners here have more room for stables and corrals for horses, as well as easier access to the bridle trails. Some have groves of orange or avocado trees surrounding the estate house.

This loop is a bit more open, which gives rubbernecking drivers a better opportunity to glimpse the 5,000-square-foot ranch house at the top of the hill.

Cross the golf course, then follow its northern edge before going into the hills and past the San Dieguito Reservoir.

- **START**: Paseo Delicias and La Granada. Go north on La Granda.
- Right at Avenida De Acacias.
- Left at Via De La Cumbre.
- Left at San Elijo.
- Right at Via De Fortuna.
- Right at El Montevideo.
- Right at Paseo Delicias and return to Village.

Golf carts, horses and pedestrians mix with traffic.

 # For Nature Lovers

- Lots of trees, shady driving.
- Bridal and hiking trails.
- Walking tour of village.

 # Stuff for Adults

- Check out the shops in the village.
- Dine in the restaurants.
- Stay at or just walk around the Inn at Rancho Santa Fe.

Sites and Eats

- *Find links to these web sources online at* www.joyride.guru/booklinks
- Lillian Rice and Rancho Santa Fe history, search at San Diego History Center.

Nothing like a day spent wandering around Rancho Santa Fe.

- Rancho Santa Fe Historical Society, 6036 La Flecha, Rancho Santa Fe, CA 92067. Offices in the La Flecha House, the first home of architect Lilian Rice. Open Tuesday-Friday only, as of this writing. Website has extensive information on the Rancho Santa Fe—Hollywood connection.
- The Inn at Rancho Santa Fe, 5951 Linea Del Cielo, Rancho Santa Fe, CA 92067. Historic hotel, one of the first businesses in the evolving development, built by the Santa Fe Land Improvement Company.
- Thyme in the Ranch, 16905 Avenida De Acacias, Rancho Santa Fe, CA 92091. A cute little bakery and deli right across from the park and Inn.
- Mille Fleurs, 6009 Paseo Delicias, Rancho Santa Fe, CA 92067. Legendary California French restaurant.

Along the trail.

Off-the-Grid Journey

ANZA-BORREGO'S TWO BLAIR VALLEYS HAVE TRACES OF NATIVES, 20TH CENTURY IDEALIST

Easy, off-pavement drive on the western edge of Anza-Borrego Desert State Park is good for off-road novices with all-wheel-drive vehicles. Spectacular desert vistas along 8-mile driving route in sand. Driving, hiking trails are well marked; primitive camping available. Location is down Banner Grade from Julian, close to metropolitan San Diego County.

Unique desert flora.

🛡 Your Journey

IF HISTORY IS JUST records of a memory, here's a trip where to-day's drivers can make their own history, while experiencing the remnants of someone else's memories.

It's well worth the more than 90-minute trip each way from central San Diego to Blair Valley and Little Blair Valley in Anza-Borrego Desert State Park. There, a drive on a trail and a few hikes take visitors to see ancient Native American art and artifacts, plus the remains of a depression-era dream to live "off the grid."

Along a trail about eight miles long (more with some of the side trails), that begins and ends along county Highway S-2, are two significant Native American archaeological sites and the former Marshal South homestead. The history runs from more than 2,000 years ago to the era of the Great Depression in the last century.

This is one of those "getting there is half the fun" drives, as you'll wind through San Diego County's prime backcountry to get to the desert. Find your best route to the old gold mining town of Julian, then go northeast through town, following the signs to Banner Grade and Borrego Springs via state Highway 78. Enjoy the twists and turns of Banner Grade and the rest of your mountain journey.

AT THE BOTTOM OF Banner Grade, Highway 78 straightens out in the desert, leading to the first major junction, with county Highway S-2, at Scissors Crossing. Bear right onto S-2, heading south (Interstate 8 is a long way away) to the small settlement of Shelter Valley. When I visited, the Stagecoach Trails RV Horse and Camping Resort, operated by the same family that owns Santee's Pure Flo Water Company, had upgraded the campground (for people, horses, and RVs) and the small market. If you haven't had lunch yet or need supplies, stop in.

After passing Shelter Valley, leave S-2 at either Little Blair Valley Road, about two miles south of Shelter Valley, or Blair Valley Road, farther south. Whether you're coming or going, you'll be driving on S-2, a very historic highway. In between the entrances to the Blair trail, S-2 curves through a pass created by the Mormon Battalion of the 1846 Mexican-American War. Named the Great Overland Stage

Drive distances from Little Blair Valley entrance at S-2.

Route of 1849, today's S-2 was the route of the Butterfield Stage used by none other than Author Mark Twain, who described his journey in his 1872 book, *Roughing It*.

It was also the Southern Emigrant Trail, in the days before railroads, and a route used by Spanish explorer Juan Bautista de Anza in 1774. All were headed from Arizona or Mexico to coastal California. The dirt trail traverses a ridge that separates the two valleys; to the west, S-2 runs through a pass where the Mormon Battalion blazed the trail.

IT'S EASY TO MISS the turn to Little Blair Valley—the entrance to Blair Valley is easier to find, with a larger sign at S-2 and a restroom hut visible from the highway; either way you go, you will end up back at S-2. It's about eight miles of sandy road that is easy to navigate in most of today's all-wheel-drive SUVs.

Here's a place where you can make your own memories while exploring history. Most SUV drivers don't ever take their vehicle off the pavement—in this case onto a generally graded, sandy trail. This route is one where you can have an enjoyable day and get your tires dirty.

For explorers new to the local deserts, the area, also known as the Ghost Mountain and Box Canyon regions of Anza-Borrego, aren't something out of the old Star Wars scenes with R2D2 and C3PO crossing the dunes (those scenes were shot about 100 miles east at the Algondones Dunes). This area is sandy canyon bottom with rugged granitic rock-covered hills.

Watch for Little Blair Valley entry south of mile marker 22.

Dry lake provides spectacular vistas.

AGAVE AND OTHER succulents, along with ocotillo and a few grasses cover the sand, meaning bugs and birds and other animals are around. These food sources are probably why humans have been living here for thousands of years, leading to the area being declared a cultural preserve. In wet years, look for flowers blooming in the spring.

Local author Diana Lindsay, in her book *Anza-Borrego A to Z*, reports that the valleys were named either after "Bronco Sam Blair" or murdered prospector David Blair.

The well-marked trail makes for fun driving on the generally sandy roads. Even novice dirt-road drivers will enjoy the challenge of maneuvering on the loose soil while observing the unique desert flora and the rugged mountains framing the valley.

Take it easy on the sand and keep your speed down. The road is one-lane in many spots, with turnouts here and there for passing. It can be very surprising to climb to the top of one of the small ridges along the route and see another vehicle coming your way. The rule on one-lane roads is that the uphill car backs up to where it can turn out.

The driving fun (and challenges) come from the variety of terrain along the trail, including wide open sandy areas and ridges that need to be traversed. There are several spots where the desert brush comes right up to the narrow trail as it twists and turns. The Colorado Desert, which runs east from San Diego's Laguna Mountain range, has great geologic diversity.

IF YOU THINK YOU'RE in the middle of nowhere on Highway S-2, you'll really feel like you're away from it all after a mile or so on the trail. Even though there are many narrow spots, just drive a little further and there'll be a turnout or impromptu parking area. Stop for a bit and just experience the desert.

I cruised around for a couple of hours, taking the side trips up to all the sites and drove about 13 miles. It's the kind of drive that almost any vehicle can take. While several Jeep Wranglers and even an old CJ-7 were out on the trail during my visit, other drivers had chosen a Toyota Prius, Pontiac Vibe, and even a Mini Hardtop to make the trip.

For a little exercise, take any of the hikes to the three archaeological sites along the route, each about a mile's walk from a parking area. One of those sites belonged to a person who seriously experienced the desert, an early off-gridder by the name of Marshal South, who brought his family here in 1930. An artist and author, South picked for his homestead a waterless mountaintop at the south end of today's drive. Take the Yaquitapec Trail, where a hike up the hill takes you to the ruins of the home. KPBS-TV has a great interview with South's son, Rider, from 2013.

In the middle of the drive is the 'Ehmuu-Morteros Trail, which runs through a one-time Kumeyaay village. Artifacts include cuples (grinding holes in the rocks), an ancient Kumeyaay food preparation area, and pictographs.

JUST NORTH OF THE 'Ehmuu-Morteros Trail parking area, the road splits.

Directional signs can be tough to find but don't mess up the view.

Take the northeast trail to the turn to the Pictograph Ghost Mountain Road, and then to the mile-long Pictograph Trail. Here, ancient humans painted symbols on the rocks—diamonds, zigzags, suns, and other figures—whose meanings have been lost in time.

Finally, a word about supplies. Although some civilization is only a few miles away, this is a place where visitors should bring plenty of water. The desert air has very low humidity and folks get thirsty very quickly. The summer heat speaks for itself, but temperatures can climb past the century mark as early as May and as late as October. Be sure to make all the preparations they taught you in elementary school… water, sunscreen, snacks, etc. Even if it's a warm day, bring jackets, as once the sun falls behind the Laguna Mountains, the temperature drops quickly. Oh, and make sure the car or truck is in good shape.

Memories are made of experiences and journeys. Making your own memories and sharing in the history of other explorers makes this trip well worth the drive.

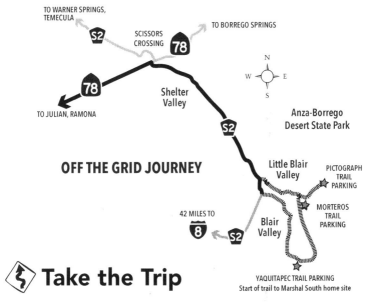

Take the Trip

DISTANCE: 8-13 miles, depending on side trails taken. Blair Valley is about 75 miles from central San Diego via SR-78 or SR-79 through Julian.

DIFFICULTY: Challenging curves on SR-78 and SR-79 through the mountains. Easy to moderate on sand, depending on conditions on Blair Valley Road, Little Blair Valley Road, and other trails.

DIRECTIONS
- *See Google Map:* http://goo.gl/KriODK
- Take your best route to Julian. Depending on your starting point, head north from East County on Interstate 8 east to SR-79 north, or SR-67 north and SR-78 east to the mountain town of Julian. From Central or North County, your route is SR-78 east to Julian through Ramona, or from I-15 south of Escondido, east over

Scripps-Poway Parkway to SR-67 north, and SR-78 east through Ramona.

- Continue on SR-78 east to the desert.
- Right at county Highway S-2 (south), the Great Overland Stage Route of 1849.
- Left at Little Blair Valley Road, approximately ¼-mile south of mile marker 22. If you miss this turn, look for Blair Valley Road approximately ½-mile south of mile marker 23.

 For Nature Lovers

- Desert wilderness experience.
- Three hiking trails.
- Desert flora and fauna.
- Spectacular granitic hills.

Sites and Eats

- *Find links to these web sources online at* www.joyride.guru/booklinks
- Little Blair Valley Cultural Preserve map. Includes trails.
- Marshal South and the Anza-Borrego Desert State Park, interview with Rider South (his son) from KPBS-TV.
- Excerpt from John McDonald documentary on Ghost Mountain.
- Federal Highway Administration history of Great Overland Stage Route of 1849.

Trail to former Marshal South home.

Borrego Badlands from Font's Point.

Beautiful Badlands

A TWISTING JOURNEY FROM THE PACIFIC TO ANZA-BORREGO DESERT STATE PARK AND SPECTACULAR FONTS POINT

Drive from the ocean to the desert, through the city, mountains, and the desert town of Borrego Springs, ending at Fonts Point for spectacular views of San Diego County's unique ecosystem. It's a challenging drive after leaving urban San Diego County and an all-wheel or four-wheel drive vehicle is recommended for the loose-sand road to Fonts Point.

Road to Font's Point.

◯ Your Journey

A DRIVE FROM THE BLUE Pacific Ocean through 6,000-foot mountains to the tranquility of the desert in about two hours is one of unique features of San Diego County.

Two major highways run east from within a mile of the beach, through the mountains and to the desert. In central San Diego, you're at Ocean Beach, near the western terminus of Interstate 8, which runs from here to Casa Grande, Arizona, about 350 miles east. Or, you're in northern San Diego County, at Oceanside, near the western end of state Route 78, which goes 225 miles east to Blythe, California, on the Arizona border.

We're not driving that far today. The goal in this journey is to explore a jewel—the second-largest state park in the US—the 600,000-acre Anza-Borrego Desert State Park, and Fonts Point Overlook, just east of the town of Borrego Springs.

This is a route that can be done (roundtrip) on a long day or over a weekend, with an overnight of camping or hotels in the desert or mountains. Whatever your choice, it's a way to explore the desert without getting too far away from civilization.

An all-wheel-drive or four-wheel-drive vehicle is recommended due to the sandy conditions on the Fonts Point Wash. To get there, each route takes a beautiful path through the Laguna Mountains. Via SR-78, you'll experience the citrus groves and vistas of the San Pasqual Valley. Over Interstate 8 and SR-79, the road twists through Cuyamaca Rancho State Park and past Lake Cuyamaca.

The meeting point for both routes from the beach is the mountain town of Julian. The road from Oceanside is easy—just follow SR-78 east. From Ocean Beach and central San Diego on Interstate 8, take the Descanso/Japatul Road/SR-79 exit and follow the signs through Cuyamaca to Julian.

BOTH ROUTES INVOLVE SOME serious hairpin turns and mountain driving so take your time and enjoy the views. From Julian, head down Banner Grade, which quickly descends into the western end of Anza-Borrego Desert State Park. Once on the desert floor, watch for the signs to Borrego Springs and Yaqui Pass Road. On the other side of this sometimes twisty pass is Borrego Springs, a small desert town with a few shops, restaurants, and hotels. The Borrego Art Institute is on Christmas Circle, in a restored mid-century modern building that was once a grocery store.

The park's visitor center, at the west end of Palm Canyon Drive, is a good spot to find out about road conditions and the area's history. The Anza-Borrego Foundation's small museum is also a "must visit." Both venues have knowledgeable staff and volunteers who can answer all your questions about the desert and your journey.

Follow county Highway S-22 east about 10 miles (it turns and changes names a couple of times) to the Fonts Point trail. Whether you're a first-timer off road or a veteran desert rat, you're in for a treat.

The road to Fonts Point shows much of the variety that is a desert ecosystem. It ranges from a wide wash to a few narrow, hilly spots. You'll experience mini-dunes and see volcanic fields, wind- and wa-

Welcome to Borrego Springs.

Don't miss the sign from the highway.

ter-scarred cliffs, and wide open vistas all in the four miles to the point.

STAY ON THE WELL-MARKED trail. The sand is squishy and fun to drive on, but take it easy as you probably will see other drivers on the road (if you want to traverse dunes, keep driving east to Glamis).

For the true eco-tourist, select an all-wheel drive hybrid vehicle that allows all-electric mode (usually up to 15-20 mph). I've taken a hybrid SUV on drives in the desert and the effect is enchanting. There's no sound but the sand crunching under the tires; not much noisier than if you were hiking.

But any AWD or 4WD vehicle will have a good time on the sand. Many drivers in the San Diego area choose these cars, trucks and SUVs for their advantages in ice, snow, and rain. However, in most parts of Southern California, we don't have any ice or snow and very little rain. The bottom line is that these buyers have paid for something they'll probably never use. Here's a chance to give it some exercise.

Stop where you can along the way to take in the solitude and big sky (sorry, Montana) of a unique spot in Southern California. At the end of the trail, there's a parking area, a short hike away from the edge of the Borrego Badlands and an unbelievable view.

The Borrego Badlands are several hundred square miles where, over the centuries, wind and water have carved out the bottom of what was once an inland sea. The spectacular vista – Fonts Point – overlooks something that's been described as a "miniature Grand Canyon." Five million years of exposed sediments include layers from the Pliocene and Pleistocene epochs. The result is a landscape of dramatic colors; geology aficionados call it the best place in North America to view this look back into history. Desert explorer Jim Bremner has a great YouTube video featuring a drone flyover of Fonts Point.

Fonts Point is named for Father Pedro Font, the chaplain and scribe for Juan Bautista de Anza's 1774-75 expedition across California (scouting a route to the Spanish settlements on the coast). Accounts say Font described the point as the "sweepings of the earth." It was named for Font in the 1930s by a local developer; De Anza's party isn't known to have visited this spot. Some of the roads in the area are marked for the National Park Service's Juan Bautista de Anza Historic Trail, which runs from Nogales, Arizona, to the San Francisco Bay area.

PLAN TO SPENT SOME time at Fonts Point. Although there is no shade and no services, the view, a hundred feet or more above the canyon floor, is worth taking in unhurried. In the spring, the plants around are green and—although it's not the best spot—visitors can spot some of the park's famous desert flower bloom. The heat sets in during April and May, and things don't cool off until November. If you come in summer, bring plenty of water.

On a clear day, the view reaches all the way to Mexico, more than 40 miles away. At various times in geologic history, this area has been

All-wheel or front-wheel drive recommended.

Short hike to Font's Point.

at the bottom of the Colorado River and Gulf of California. The Anza-Borrego Desert Natural History Association has a brochure of a driving tour the length of the Borrego-Salton Seaway called "Erosion Road." It gives drivers a perspective on the rugged hills and gorges in the area.

It is a popular spot, so you'll likely see other travelers at the trail's end. It's okay to bring in your own supplies and have a picnic, but you'll need to bring along your own chairs if you don't want to sit in the car or on the ground. Supplies are available in several spots along the way, including Borrego Springs, where there's a small but well-stocked grocery store. There are also several restaurants in Borrego Springs. Check online services for up-to-date reviews.

DESERT RATS NEVER return without a big bag of pink grapefruit, grown right around Borrego Springs. The local Kiwanis Club sells it right in Christmas Circle in the center of town, or, if the shack is closed, head over to the market just to the west.

On the way back, there's more locally grown goodies to be had if you follow SR-78. Santa Ysabel, just down the hill from Julian, is home to Dudley's Bakery, a local landmark by any definition. Since 1963, it's been a must-stop spot for pie and other goodies either going or coming to the mountains. Next door is Don's Market, which makes its own sausage and has a specialty meat counter that sometimes includes locally raised bison.

The next stop is what everybody calls the "egg place in Ramona," actually the Pine Hill Egg Ranch's tiny retail outlet, at 25818 California 78, Ramona. On a recent trip, we picked up a couple of dozen eggs, the final ingredient for a fresh, local breakfast back at home.

From Ramona, follow SR-67 south if your destination is central San Diego—to head back to I-8, just stay on 67; to go to Interstate 15, go west at Scripps-Poway Parkway. Otherwise, follow SR-78 back to

Oceanside, via Escondido, San Marcos, and Vista.

The moral of this story is if you've paid for all-wheel drive, get out and use it. The drive to Font's Point is one of the easiest anywhere that will challenge that AWD transfer case you not only paid for, but have been hauling around all these years. And it will take you to one of the most spectacular views on earth.

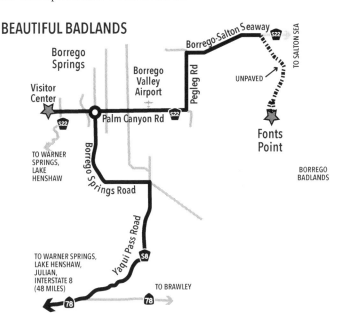

BEAUTIFUL BADLANDS

Take the Trip

DISTANCE: Approximately 103 miles round-trip from central San Diego, 105 miles from Oceanside.

DIFFICULTY: Moderate, with twisting mountain roads over and back, plus sandy road to Fonts Point. All-wheel or four-wheel-drive vehicle recommended.

DIRECTIONS
- *See Google Map: https://goo.gl/nQfU6A*
  FROM CENTRAL SAN DIEGO
- Interstate 8 to SR-79 (Descanso). North on SR-79.
- Follow signs past Descanso Junction to stay on SR-79/Cuyamaca-Julian

FROM NORTHERN SAN DIEGO COUNTY
- Follow SR-78 east to Escondido, Ramona, and Julian.

FROM JULIAN
- In Julian, right at Banner Road/SR-78.
- Left at Yaqui Pass Road.
- Keep left to Deep Well Trail.
- At Christmas Circle traffic roundabout, follow east exit to county S-22. Follow road (the name changes to Pegleg Road then Borrego Salton Seaway) about 10 miles to Fonts Point entrance.

RETURN TRIP VIA RAMONA
- Return to SR-78 and follow signs to Ramona. Continue on SR-78 to Escondido and I-15. Optional southbound route via SR-67 to Lakeside and I-8, or Scripps-Poway Parkway west to I-15.

For Nature Lovers

- Spectacular vistas at Fonts Point
- Short hike to viewing points.
- Sandy driving can be fun.
- Good introduction to desert ecosystem.
- Buy local eggs, meat, fruit and vegetables for tomorrow's dinner.

Stuff for Kids

- Short hike to Fonts Point.
- Clean desert air.
- Definitely not a commercial theme park.
- Interactive displays at Visitor Center.

Sites and Eats

- *Visit the Joyride Guru website at* www.joyride.guru/booklinks *for live links to these locations.*
- Anza-Borrego Desert State Park official site
- Video trip to Fonts Point
- Anza Borrego Foundation
- Desert explorer Jim Bremner's video of drone flyover of Fonts Point
- Juan Bautista de Anza Historic Trail
- Dudley's Bakery, Santa Ysabel
- Don's Market, Santa Ysabel
- Pine Hill Egg Ranch, 25818 SR-78, Ramona.

Other Books by Jack Brandais

Individual drives in this series are available in the Amazon Kindle fo[r]mat through Amazon.com. The Kindle-format drives have live links a[nd] other special features available in a digital format. To download the drive[s] search on your Kindle device or app for "Joyride Guru."

• **Mulholland Madness:** Famous with motorcyclists and gearhea[ds] worldwide, explore a route over the Santa Monica Mountains with cha[l]lenging, twisting roads, movie history, hiking trails and spectacular view[s] on the way over the 3,000-foot mountains from Agoura Hills to Malibu [in] the northwest corner of Los Angeles County.

• **Weekend Driver San Diego:** In 2003, "Weekend Driver" column[ist] Jack Brandais put his favorite drives together in a "must have" collection th[at] will allow everyone from newcomers to natives to explore our diverse cou[n]ty and its intriguing environs. From Point Loma to Anza-Borrego Dese[rt] State Park, from Baja California's Guadalupe Valley to Huntington Beac[h], Brandais has found some of the best roads—paved and unpaved, twisty a[nd] straight. A true driving enthusiast, he really knows his stuff, whether it [is] the best type of vehicle for each drive, the type of scenery to expect, or abo[ut] how long it will take to complete.

About the Author

Award-winning author Jack Brandais, the Joyride Guru, has been dri[v]ing or riding on roads around San Diego County since he was a kid: Sunday drives with his dad or mom at the wheel.

Actually a third-generation road fan, his grandmother—a pioneer driving enthusiast—first explored these roads back in the 1920s.

This background has lead him to create the Joyride Guru rides. They're all great day trips... sometimes a long day trip if you decide to ex-plore.

After creating 10 drives around San Diego for Amazon Kindle, the first print book of the series, *Joyrides Around San D[i]ego*, has been released.

He's expanding the series outside of San Diego County; the first tit[le] *Mulholland Madness*, takes drivers and riders on a tour of the spectacul[ar] movie and TV location-favorite, the Santa Monica Mountains in weste[rn] Los Angeles County.

Since 2000, he's been the award-winning Weekend Driver column[ist] for *San Diego Union-Tribune* newspaper's auto section, taking readers o[n] great roads around Southern California and reviewing a new car. His pr[e]vious book, *Weekend Driver San Diego*, was published by Sunbelt Books [in] 2003.

Check out his award-winning website at *www.joyride.guru*

Made in the USA
San Bernardino, CA
20 February 2017